THE HEALING ROAD

Meditations on Life in Medicine

Brian Sayers, MD

W_PB

Writing Brave LLC

1940 Palmer Avenue, #1032
Larchmont NY 10538

www.writingbravepress.com

Distributed by IngramSpark

Copyright ©2026 by Brian Sayers, MD

All the necessary due diligence has been made to contact the copyright holders. Anyone who believes that their copyright to be infringed upon is welcome to contact the publisher.

All rights reserved. No part of this book may be reproduced in any form or by any electronic or mechanical means, including information storage and retrieval systems, without written permission from the author, except by a reviewer who may quote passages for review.

Cover and Text Design: Melissa Williams Design LLC

Copyeditor: Meghan Muldowney

Author Photos: Chad W Adams Photography

Library of Congress Cataloging-in-Publication Data available.

ISBN 979-8-9918111-5-6 (Paperback)
ISBN 979-8-9918111-6-3 (eBook)

First Edition

This book is provided for educational and informational purposes only and does not constitute providing medical advice or professional services. The information provided should not be used for diagnosing or treating a health problem or disease. Always seek the advice of your doctor or other qualified health provider regarding a medical or mental health condition. You should not disregard professional medical advice or delay in seeking it because of something you have read in this book. No physician-patient relationship is created by this book or its use. Neither the author or publisher, nor their employees, nor any contributor to this book, makes any representations, express or implied, with respect to the information provided herein or to its use.

All copyrights to the book and its contents are the property of the author unless otherwise noted. No one may reproduce, distribute or display copies of content material without the prior express permission of the author.

For Maryann, the love of my life

...and for my colleagues and patients who I have greatly admired, learned from, been inspired by.

Table of Contents

Introduction   1

First Steps

Stealing Fire   13
Simplicity   19
Harvest   24
Three Bridges   29

The Things We Carry

Healing   39
My Friend Richard   45
The 109th Bead   50
The Snow Storm   55

Turning into the Storm

Turning into the Storm   63
Calling   68
Faith   73
Love   81
Courage   85

Scenery

The Acorn   93
Let It Be   98
The Bear   102

Companions on the Trail

The Dump Truck	109
Lost in Translation	114
Kinship, Tenderness, and Being Rescued	120

Recovery

Recovery	129
Letting Go	134
In the Gloaming	139

Trail Markers

Caduceus	145
Homecomings . . . and Getting Flipped	149
Hippocrates Shrugged	155
True North	160
A River Runs Through It	165
Unleashed	170
Medicine as a Spiritual Practice	175
Standing on Holy Ground	180

Firm Footing

Writing a Wrong	187
Three Trout and Wisdom From the Ordinary	192
The Imposter	197
Mending Wall	203

Goliath	208
The Cosmic Dance	213
Herzensbildung	217
The Fourfold Path: Telling the Story	222
A Flight to Nowhere	227
Wabi-Sabi	231
The Junk Drawer	236

In the Wilderness

The Space Between the Notes	243
Extroverts, Tortured Poets, and the Long Journey	246
A View From Section 5	251
Regret	256
The Antidote to Shame	263
Broken Open	269
A Train in the Distance	274
Hope Floats	282
Miracle Shall Follow Miracle	286

Pilgrim

Pilgrimage	293
Finisterre	299

Afterword — 305
Acknowledgments — 315

Introduction

All good stories begin with a creation story—an origin story. It's true of ancient civilizations that told stories of monsters, dueling gods, and the chaos of nature. Stories of cosmic eggs hatching, of the coalescence of vapors, pieces of light, or matter to form the earth, gods, or living beings. Native American creation stories involve bald eagles, taming or navigating the chaos of nature, a quest for fire. Religions have creation stories which form the earliest stories of how humans encountered God. Marriages have creation stories of how we met, how the proposal took place, what went wrong or right at the wedding ceremony—all of which are recounted to friends and family in the decades that follow, if we're lucky. Friendships have creation stories, a history that is embedded in the friendship giving it a lasting foundation.

    Anyone who makes the commitment to a life

in medicine has a creation story, the story of how they heard their calling, then found a way to follow it. I am a baby boomer, a child of the '60s, which was still an era when doctors were greatly admired, sometimes even idolized. I grew up in awe of doctors, witnessing doctor-heroes on TV and in my own vividly remembered encounters with my pediatrician and those who cared for family members. I watched our next door neighbor, an allergist, in his tailored suits, with his perfect family, sports cars, boat, and lake house. In my childhood dreams and make-believe games, unlike my friends, I was more likely to be a doctor than a sheriff or a combat soldier.

When I was twelve, though a child's eyes, I watch my father suffer hepatic failure and death from alcoholism. The whole family suffered along with him. It was hard to make sense of all that was going on, and I wouldn't piece together the truth about his death until I was in medical school. But I was fascinated by the doctors taking care of him, and the care that he received, often watching them discuss his condition in whispered tones with my mother. Two decades later, the internist who cared for my father in Austin would become my own patient. I would care for his severe rheumatoid disease and later diagnose his widely metastatic cancer.

I attended medical school at Southwestern Medical School in Dallas before doing an internal medicine residency in the desert of New Mexico at the county hospital and regional VA hospital in Albuquerque. Any doctor reading this will know what life-changing years those can be, for me both becoming a real doctor but also becoming a fully formed adult, husband, and father. I still remember many of those patients almost a half century later, as well as my time spent with mentors and fellow residents, all of whom gave me gifts that I carry, remember, and use to this very day.

After a rheumatology fellowship in the mid-1980s, my wife, son, and I moved back to Austin. I practiced at a large multi-specialty clinic for a brief eighteen months before realizing that while I loved the collegiality, I didn't love having sixty-eight bosses. In the years that followed, I practiced solo for a decade, then solo or in small partnerships.

Our family grew in those early years of practice: a son and two daughters. While I could say there were all the challenges of practicing medicine and having a family, the truth is that in that in those days "work/life integration" was not a concept. Working too hard was a badge of honor, a product of the poor example of my esteemed mentors from an earlier era in medicine. Yes, we were given both pearls and "black pearls" from those who taught us how to practice medicine.

As I approached my fifties, my wife was diagnosed with a spinal cord tumor. In the years that followed, despite the best efforts of her many doctors, her disease left her paraplegic. I struggled as many do in midlife, working too many hours, with a young child still at home. Maybe it was burnout or depression or just the sense that important questions about life were just not being answered. I spent five years—evenings and weekends—studying at an Episcopal seminary near our home, never finding all the answers I sought, but finding a certain footing, certainly finding faith. To some extent, I found a kind of calm, acceptance, and patience that, while still a struggle, I don't think I would have found any other way. In those same years, during a time of both struggle and unexpected renewal, through grace I was given a new kind of faith and new relationships with my family, my colleagues, my work... and myself. I share these parts of my own pilgrimage to give context to the essays that follow.

In the years after seminary, I worked with men recently released from prison living in transitional housing, doing Bible study, and discussing reentry, their troubled pasts, and hopes for the future. Yes, even they are propelled by hope, often for the simplest things. I volunteered for many years at a clinic that cares for undocumented immigrants, admiring their patience and resilience, and finding them to be incredibly grateful for the care we give them. For a decade, I worked with unhoused men at a residential drug and alcohol recovery center in an older part of town so often ignored by their more affluent neighbors across town. I came to respect these men, learned valuable lessons from them, and more fully realized how the cards we are dealt at birth can make all the difference. At some point, this morphed into a realization that I might develop a better connection with my colleagues in my own medical family in some way. I eventually co-founded a nonprofit through our 4,500-member county medical society that provides free, anonymous counseling for physicians in need. I became chair of the committee that supports and advocates for our colleagues in recovery. These activities have been life changing for me, have given me much more than I have given, and for that I am grateful.

The trajectory of my own life was shaped by these and many other events and people. We all have stories that propel us to do—for better or worse—the things that we do in life. Confronting how these things affect you and your behavior later in life is one of the great challenges of adulthood when so much history starts to add up.

In more recent years since we started our counseling program for our medical family in Austin, we started publishing a weekly Sunday morning e-mail for my colleagues with news about our program, resources for personal and professional well-being, and essays written by me and some of my colleagues. As I write this book, our weekly open rate is about 3,000. The e-mail list generates a sense of community and family, and a dialogue each week that has been very helpful in creating an atmosphere where physician wellness and counseling can be openly discussed. Over a period of seven years, I have written scores of essays and in this book have published those that were received the best by my colleagues.

These essays draw from the wisdom of some people whom I greatly admire and whose writing has been a source of inspiration, comfort, or much-needed wisdom. Rachel Naomi Remen, David Whyte, Mary Oliver, Thomas Merton, Henri Nouwen, Gregory Boyle, Kate Bowler, Brené Brown, Daniel Sulmasy, and John O'Donohue are among these wise and learned people. I have made every effort to credit them for their ideas and quotes, and I have listed references to encourage further reading of their work. My goal is to review or expand on some of those timeless themes, with a transformational goal of applying their wisdom to physician well-being, in order to make it accessible to my colleagues. Our program was started a few years before the pandemic. That was timely as our counseling and recovery missions were much needed in those days, and while several of the essays were written during the pandemic, I have selected the ones that carry messages still relevant today.

The essays make frequent reference to our county medical society's counseling program and our physician recovery program, and I hope this will be taken as encouragement for each of you to support similar work within your own medical community, which is, wherever you practice, indeed a family. While my experience and volunteer work has made physicians the focus of this book, I hope that my much admired healthcare partners—physician assistants, nurses, hospital and practice administrators—can connect with these essays as well. It is also written with the hope that patients (we are all patients at some point) will appreciate and find some insight into our work.

These essays tell much about my own life, a life which is entirely unique, but which also shares many of the common struggles that we all deal with. My life has been rich and full of joy, family, and work that I love, and for that I am grateful each and every day. Each of our lives and our experiences are unique and sacred, yet also part of a common pilgrimage. The work that we do is difficult, often frustrating, but when infused with patience, empathy, and love, it is incredibly rewarding and nourishing. I love practicing medicine, and I love my medical family. I hope that it shows through in this writing and will encourage reflection as you read. I hope that it conveys my sense of admiration and encouragement for you and the work you do.

FIRST STEPS

Stealing Fire

I love creation stories. Fully understood and embraced, creation stories lay a foundation for the story that follows, help us make sense of our actions, give the story context, and tell us when we are true to our roots, when we overcome them, why sometimes we are captive to them. It's true of sacred writing, popular fiction, classic literature, even campfire stories. It's true of love stories, friendships, marriage, our life's work. It's true of serious illness when our patients try to make sense of what has happened to them. It's true when we as physicians explore our calling, mistakes, triumphs, passions, and our meaningful relationships. It's true of our stories that end in tragedy. All the important stories we tell and hear have an origin. Those of us who really listen to patients know that the significance of illness lies in the human experience, in the narrative of what illness means to us. We know the importance of hearing a patient's perception of where their illness originated—the creation story of their illness.

Dr. Lewis Mehl-Madrona is a Native American physician and author of the *Coyote Trilogy*. He is a firm believer in the importance of the blending of what he describes as the bio-psycho-social-spiritual realms of illness in medical practice. His Native American roots inform him of the importance of the creation story—storytelling that is a crucial way of defining cultures, families, individuals, and even illnesses. He notes that, "Stories contain and convey the meanings and values of our lives . . . give us cultural identity . . . tell us about families and lives and what it means to belong. They comfort and heal us, both in the listening and the telling."

Creation stories of civilizations or cultures often start with mystery, with darkness, chaos and uncertainty. They sometimes start with innocence, with a search, with darkness turning to light, with struggle, and often with inconsistent progress and confusion. In Genesis, we are given a glimpse of this darkness, of raw mystery waiting to be molded, of the uneven progress of Adam and Eve, naked and ashamed, their story setting the stage for all that follows, their legacy echoing forever. I am fascinated by Mehl-Madrona's telling of the Cherokee creation legend, a hero's journey to spark the beginning of a timeless culture. Their story tells of their earliest ancestors' quest to locate and steal fire hidden on a faraway island, something essential to their survival, integral to their creation story and therefore to their future. The story of stealing fire is a story of courage and purpose that not only served their immediate needs, but also gave birth to an entire civilization. Stealing fire is a mythical image of grasping and molding your future story. As part of their healing power, medicine men in the culture that followed explored, revealed, and harvested the power of creation stories of their patient's illness to bring healing.

    Mehl-Madrona believes that nothing is more powerful in medicine than storytelling. It does not replace science or technology, but it shares an equal footing for those who truly practice the healing arts. Encouraging patients to tell the story of how their illness began in their own way and on their own terms can be a powerful tool in determining their path to healing. He notes that from a patient's perspective, "Creation stories are also important because the final story about how you or I got well must be compatible with the story about how we got sick, or the treatment will never work."

The physician distress/moral injury/burnout that many physicians suffer in some ways is an illness of the soul. Mehl-Madrona's belief in the importance of exploring creation stories to make sense of illness applies as well here as anywhere else he describes it. Creation stories change with telling and retelling. They evolve, mature, and become more interpretable, aided by those who help us through generous listening. The telling and retelling of a story of illness or trauma or distress is therapeutic in and of itself, but the story only makes sense with a clear vision of its origin. When deeply discussed with our patients or colleagues, many of them have a firmly held idea of the origin of their illness or distress. Whether the specifics of their stories make sense to us or not, it is an important starting point in the healing process for them and should therefore be explored.

Hearing the stories of others promotes healing for the listener as well. Particularly important and useful to all of us is hearing stories of transformation—of journeys from places of darkness into new life, a journey then envisioned by the listener. Stories of transformation from illness to restored health, whether physical or spiritual, are critical components of any healing journey sometimes shared between us and our patients. As Mehl-Madrona notes, "If we hear enough stories about profound transformation, we find ourselves transforming, even in spite of ourselves."

Understanding our personal creation story helps us to make sense of the origins of things that trouble us. It helps us understand illness, traumas, or challenges better so that a path to healing can be envisioned. We each have a creation story that propels us, a story that one way or another will be lived out. It is our own unique story through which we may discover the origins of the journey that brought us to the place we currently inhabit, for better or worse. Hidden within our creation story is the possibility of transformation, waiting to be discovered. There is a story to be told. There is fire to steal.

Suggested Reading

Books

Mehl-Madrona, Lewis. *Coyote Wisdom: The Power of Story in Healing*. Simon & Schuster, 1998.

Poetry

Edge, Mary Allen. "Beginnings." *Poetry*, edited by Harriet Monroe, 1923.

O'Donohue, John. "For a New Beginning." *To Bless the Space Between Us: A Book of Blessings,* Doubleday, 2008.

Scripture

The Bible, *Genesis 1:1-5, 8-13*

Simplicity

If you are a child of the 1960s, chances are your mother or grandmother made some of your clothes from scratch. They would go to a fabric store, look through the hundreds of small packets of printed sewing patterns, and select their next project. The patterns were sheets of thin tissue paper containing outlines of how the fabric should be cut, with instructions on how to piece them together. My mother dabbled in this when I was young and while she is an accomplished woman, sewing was definitely not her forte. I remember some of the shirts that she made: buttons often not lining up, sleeves not quite the same length, or overall too short in length or too loose across my small shoulders. But one piece she sewed is part of my origin story in medicine.

Around the time I was in first grade, I watched the melodramatic medical show *Dr. Kildare* each week. I saw the dashing young intern look deeply into the eyes of his patients, hold their hands, and in less than an hour, elicit miraculous cures. More importantly, he was an inquisitive, sensitive, healing presence, and watching that show caused the six-year-old version of me to know that I would be a doctor.

My mother sensed this and found a pattern—Simplicity pattern number 4714, a themed set of pajamas. From this she made me an intern's smock, even stitching a crude Caduceus over the left breast. I shamelessly wore this to school more times than I can remember during first grade. At that point in my life, it wasn't that I wanted to be *like* Dr. Kildare, I actually *was* Dr. Kildare. Looking back, it was pure, innocent, naive and, yes, it was figurative and literal simplicity. Such was my pathway into medicine.

I've been thinking about this origin story lately. More than three decades into practice, with a few missteps along the way, I still love my work. I look forward to going to my small private practice each day to see my patients, our staff, and my office partner, but more and more lately, I wonder why things have gotten so hard and complicated.

The field of rheumatology has seen almost indescribable advances for which I am grateful and in awe. So how is it possible that the same system that makes it possible to cure diseased bodies can create so many obstacles to our ability to bring healing to the people with those diseases ... and to keep the healers whole? You know exactly the obstacles I'm referring to. The frustrations and hurdles that we endure—and seemingly accept—most every day even as we try our best to care about patients and maintain passion for our work.

As a profession, we are lost if we do not continually reexamine foundational things that make us and our profession what it is at its best. The foundational things that we hold dear called us to make the sacrifices it took to become physicians—core beliefs and longings that enable us to treat patients with dignity and great care. These core beliefs are our sense of calling, our values, our need for meaning; they are the sort of things that we must discern and honor, even as the importance of these is so seldom tangibly emphasized or modeled by larger forces that increasingly control our workplace. When I think back on that six-year-old version of myself,

I'm inspired by his dream, but saddened by the things that will threaten it in the decades down the road. I want to protect him, to arm him with the courage and moral strength he will need to keep the dream pure and enduring. Perhaps I did.

In his seminal work *Crossing the Unknown Sea: Work as a Pilgrimage of Identity*, David Whyte writes, "We have our work now, a work that was formed in the growing imagination of the child we once were, but the work itself has changed and made us, formed us, into something different, something perhaps good but also disturbing at the same time . . . distant now from all other voices that crowded our childhood, try to imagine what that dreaming young self would think of the strange adult we have become." That child informs us still—their dreams, the sense of calling that was forming even in those early days. In our quiet inner life, that version of us still speaks to us with their innocent wisdom, if we will only listen.

Suggested Reading

Books

Whyte, David. *Crossing the Unknown Sea: Work as a Pilgrimage of Identity.* Riverhead Books, 2001.

Poetry

Masters, Edgar Lee. "George Gray." *Spoon River Anthology,* Macmillan & Co, 1915.

Yeats, William Butler. "When You Are Old." *The Rose*, John Lane, 1893.

Harvest

In the beginning, I spent three years in Albuquerque doing an internal medicine residency, years spent at the county hospital and a regional VA. Our patients consisted in large part of folks with humble backgrounds, most with deep Spanish and/or Navajo roots. Those were good years, a time of learning how to care for people—once I figured out how to keep them alive. Strange as it sounds, one of my best memories of those days was eating on the patio of the VA cafeteria. They made the most amazing green chili stew, full of chilis softened by hours of simmering, with pork, vegetables, and spices thrown in. I looked forward to lunch throughout morning rounds. We sat together at a communal table, sharing stories about the strange cases and people we were caring for, quirky attendings, stupid mistakes, saves and codes, turfs, and lack of sleep. We were all navigating southwestern and Navajo culture with varying degrees of success. We were learning the importance of understanding people's culture in order to care for them successfully.

I soon learned that the chili harvest was the pulse of life in New Mexico. Fall in northern New Mexico was all about hot air balloons, the chili harvest, and the communal celebration of both, with morning skies full of colorful hot air balloons rising in the high desert sunrise. Throughout the state, chili farmers would proudly bring their harvest to market in tourist towns, small villages, and roadside stands, ready for cooking or decoration.

In the southern part of the state, commercial growers produced huge crops, mostly bound for Louisiana and the insides of hot sauce bottles. But in northern New Mexico, the norm was small family farms that have grown chilis for many generations. The hard labor of growing chili was an integral part of the culture, the rhythm of daily life, and an ingredient in almost every meal. These small family farms were largely owned by folks with deep roots there, many direct descendants of Spanish colonialists with strong Native American heritage. They have worked the land to pass it and their way of living down through uncounted years, their hearts beating in rhythm with the climate, with the very soil that they labor in. Deep within their culture is an identity with that soil, with its innate mystery and value, a sense of its holiness. Even a modest harvest is a great source of pride and a cause for celebration. As one chili farmer is quoted in Carmella Padilla's *The Chile Chronicles*, "My mother always used to say, 'If you plant it with joy, it will grow.'"

One day I was eating a late lunch at the VA hospital canteen after a night on call. Our attending was an older man who inhabited a wonderful, open hacienda style home outside of town in the foothills of Sandia Peak. At the end of each rotation, he would host his residents and students, introducing us to New Mexican wine as we looked over the lights of the city. He exuded calm, a trait much needed in those days, and one I have tried unsuccessfully to emulate in the years since. He walked onto the patio, bowl of stew in hand, and sat down with me.

One of our admissions the previous night was a poor, elderly chili farmer from Chama, and his large extended family brought him all those miles for care at the VA. It was an impressive sight, this tribe of modest laborers all gathered as a family to stand vigil. He had told me about his little farm and his family that night and I related some of it on rounds.

"I've always admired people like him," my attending said. "When we are at our best, we are more like them than you might think, grounded in culture and family. When you leave here, you'll take a new culture and a new family with you."

I've thought about that offhanded bit of wisdom dispensed over a bowl of green and have considered its meaning in the years since. Those chili farmers are deeply rooted in the soil, the rhythm of the seasons, and their heritage. It binds them together, gives them purpose and faith.

Along with my own heritage of faith and family that I brought to New Mexico, I added new roots, the timeless culture of medicine and healing, and I had been given a new family. That sense of culture and family, that calling, will always be there, waiting for us to return, even when we wander or forget, drawing us back, in some form or another, to what we were meant to do.

Suggested Reading

Books

Pardilla, Carmella, and Jack Parsons. *The Chile Chronicles: Tales of a New Mexico Harvest.*

Museum of New Mexico Press, 1997.

Poetry

Hughes, Langston. "My People." *The Weary Blues*, Knopf, 1926.

Marinoni, Rosa Zagnoni. "Who Are My People?" *Behind The Mask,* Henry Harrison, 1927.

Scripture

The Bible, *Acts 2:44-47*

Three Bridges

During a long lifetime, we are many different people, we live many different lives. Sometimes when we look back, we can only shake our head at our missteps, wonder where some things went that so strongly motivated us and gave us passion for a time. Some of the people who once meant so much to us are now gone or have drifted to insignificance. But as much as we change through the years, our spiritual soul connects our past to our future, even as it too evolves. This awareness of our spiritual being is the thread that weaves its way through our lives and makes us who we are. Denying or ignoring it—even failing to actively explore and nurture it throughout our lives—is the source of much of the misery so many people experience.

In the practice of medicine, a sense of spirituality is no less critical to our daily work. It is a thread that connects the stages we go through in our lives as physicians. Spirituality in medicine connects science with humanity. It transforms curing to healing. To fully understand our profession and our daily work, we must be connected on a human level with our patients, as equals—sharing suffering, joy, and love. It means that our work is a visible expression of a journey to what lies deep within the heart. Whether we fully realize it or not, the presence of spirituality is a deep need we have if we are going to love our work.

In our ever-changing understanding of our profession and its heritage, doctors more and more have been writing about the importance of spirituality in our work in recent years, driven by the rise of the physician well-being movement. This is no surprise—physician well-being is inextricably linked to spiritual health. But what is spirituality and where does it come from? We all have some sense of what spirituality is, though it is hard to put into words. It certainly includes a deep sense of interconnectedness with those around us and those who preceded us, with nature and the universe. There is a sense of something transcendent, something greater than us, moving around and within us, trying to speak to us and through us. Spirituality may be expressed and explored in many ways, only one of which is organized religion.

Most of us sense that things change in our lives when we connect with our embedded spirituality. Author Lisa Miller, Ph.D., calls this state the "awakened brain." I had a chance to hear her speak at a seminar in New Mexico one summer. Dr. Miller's premise is that for years, research scientists dismissed spirituality as a domain that lacked scientific rigor. A wide separation developed between science and spirituality. Often confusing religious agendas with spirituality, public and private institutions have shied away from stressing the importance of spirituality out of a sense of political correctness or for a perceived lack of scientific evidence proving its critical importance. But as Dr. Miller asserts, "Our individual health and flourishing depend on our choice to awaken. So do the health and flourishing of our schools, workplaces, governments—and the planet."

Dr. Miller has compiled years of research utilizing several study modalities, including brain activation mapping, genotyping, twin studies, and other rigorous scientific techniques. She notes that research increasingly recognized for its significance shows that we are "innately spiritual beings," spirituality being fully one-third innate and two-thirds environmental. Her main point is that what happens to that innate spiritual yearning we are born with, how it is nurtured (or ignored) by environment, primarily by our parents early in life, has profound and lasting effects on individual lives, and on society in general.

Her groundbreaking research demonstrates that those in whom spirituality takes firm hold are dramatically less likely to have serious depression or addiction issues, and as teenagers, they are less likely to die by suicide. Nothing else comes close to being as protective in those domains as spiritual awareness. Growing and nurturing that spiritual birthright—that basic yearning for connection and meaning—falls squarely on family. The consequences of missing the opportunity to equip our children with spiritual armor are seen by school counselors, college therapists, employers, even law enforcement. It is seen later in life with difficulty in life transitions, with burnout and mood disturbances.

Miller notes that there are "three bridges where we are hardwired to have an existential search." The most important is the bridge in adolescence but also of great consequence are the bridges into middle and old age.

Societies through millennia have recognized the adolescent bridge into adulthood as an important time to recognize physical changes, but also the important spiritual transitions that must take place. These are transitions that the soul longs for at that point in life, a spiritual awakening that is crucial for the rest of our life. Examples include: bat/bar mitzvah, confirmation, vision quest, quinceañera, the Maasai coming of age ceremony, Khatam al-Quran. Miller believes that much of what ails emerging generations today is lack of nurturing this critical juncture within families, the consequences being the epidemic of teen depression and lack of moral compass so commonly seen. She contends that what is often diagnosed and treated as depression in teens is really an unmet spiritual yearning, a lost developmental opportunity that may haunt them into adulthood. She believes this is entirely avoidable if we see ourselves as torchbearers charged with the intergenerational transmission of spiritual values.

Later, there is another surge of spiritual yearning, often called a midlife crisis, a sense of restlessness and questioning. We often conveniently blame a job that isn't ideal, a marriage that seems unfulfilling, or a perceived lack of success. However, Miller asserts that this is really a time that calls not so much for a job change or divorce (though sometimes it does), but more often for deeper examination of connectedness, meaning, and exploration of our relationship with something larger than ourselves. In our program's work with physicians, we have often noticed that the second bridge so often associated with our late forties or fifties actually occurs more often in the thirties. This is particularly true of many female physicians caught in the storm of high expectations in being married, raising children, and trying to establish a thriving medical practice against the unexpected headwinds of today's healthcare realities.

That day in the high desert spent with colleagues studying physician well-being connected some dots for me regarding teen depression, our counseling program, and my own years of middle-aged angst. I recognize now that certain phases of my adult life that I interpreted as depression or burnout were really arrival at that second bridge Dr. Miller describes, perhaps arriving there without benefit of a fully formed crossing of the first bridge all those years ago. We all sense stages of life where spiritual renewal, renewed connection—awakening—is urgent, but these transitions don't always occur as a "crisis" or some other dramatic change. In fact, I think more often these awakenings occur in small stages at those junctures. Indeed, sometimes those transitions or transformations occur so gradually, so subtly, that we only see them in retrospect, or feel a gradual unease when we sense the window is being missed. But in the end, we are hardwired for spiritual yearning and connection. It is never too late.

Suggested Reading

Blessings

O'Donohue, John. "For the Interim Time." *To Bless the Space Between Us: A Book of Blessings,* Doubleday, 2008.

Books

Buford, Bob. *Halftime: Changing Your Game Plan from Success to Significance.* Zondervan, 1995.

Miller, Lisa. *The Awakened Brain: The Psychology of Spirituality*. Penguin, 2022.

Poetry

Whyte, David. "The Journey." *The House of Belonging,* Many Rivers Press, 1997.

THE THINGS WE CARRY

Healing

In a box in my office is a cherished collection of letters and cards from patients and their families-touching messages sent to me during these past thirty-five years. There is also a list of patients who have passed away during those same years—119 names on the list now—written in my own hand with a single sentence describing each person. I thought that down the line I would need this prompt to remember them, but it turns out I don't. They are sacred memories from a lifetime spent in this office. Within this box lies the meaning I have found in my work, and I realize that that the essence of this meaning comes from a certain kind of healing that was mutually exchanged with many of those patients. Many of my current patients have been with me for more than a quarter of a century and I realize now that no matter how much I have tried to give to patients, I have received at least as much in return.

Much has been written about physician wellness in recent years, and more and more the search for meaning in our daily work has been recognized as a primary driver of physician well-being. As we dig deeper into what creates a sense of meaning in our lives as physicians, perhaps the key is healing. By this, we typically mean healing our patients, but if we're honest, we often are most connected to our work when we receive healing ourselves.

What is healing? It's almost trite to talk about curing versus healing nowadays. When our patients are sick, there are two processes present: disease (a disruption of body function) and illness (how patients experience disease, how it disrupts their lives). We increasingly recognize that curing or controlling disease is only part of our calling as physicians. It is incomplete if we ignore healing. Healing calls on us to give something of ourselves to others, a part of our heart, even if sometimes it's just as simple as listening.

Healing is sometimes described as the attainment of inner peace or a reclaiming of wholeness. Saki Santorelli wrote that healing occurs when "we feel connected, whole, filled with a sense of belonging no matter what the condition of our body." But I think it's best described by Daniel Sulmasy who notes, "Ancient people readily understood illness as a disturbance in relationships ... Illness disturbs more than relationships inside the human organism, it disrupts families and workplaces and shatters pre-existing patterns of coping." He emphasizes that in ancient cultures, people were also keenly aware of the importance of the relationship between human beings and the cosmos. The task of the ancient shaman was to heal by helping the ill restore these disrupted relationships. Perhaps that is our task as well, both within and beyond, our work as physicians.

In the long lineage of medicine, only recently has the application of science almost entirely displaced the practice of healing in our "encounters" with patients. Curing takes less effort, less time, less thought, and less patience than healing, but this emphasis was not always the norm. The roots of our proud history saw healing provided through shamans, curanderos, mystics, and ancient priests who, with limited scientific tools, knew that healing and curing are inextricably linked rather than two separate processes.

Later, care by physicians, hospitals, and other organizations was often led by religious and charitable organizations that understood that the need for healing of the heart was just as critical as the need for curing the body. This heritage of healing is becoming less and less recognizable in an era when the economics of healthcare kidnaps the agenda that too often sets aside the urgent call for healing. Anyone who really works with patients knows intuitively that we derive meaning from the healing process, both as givers and recipients, and when that is lost, so too is our sense of fulfillment and calling.

In that box in my office, on that list of patients who have passed away is the name of Patient #76. She was one of the first patients who trusted me when I opened my little practice all those years ago. We were about the same age, really just kids back then. We grew older together along with her lupus in those next two decades before she unexpectedly died. She was a friend as well as a patient, and I pray that in those years I offered her some help with healing. I know that like so many other patients, she gave me many gifts. One of the gifts was a certain kind of healing that is felt when we as physicians come to terms with our own humanity and mortality, with the limitations and imperfections that are part of our work. Healing is always possible. Even for us.

Suggested Reading

Articles

Bradford, Carol. "The Power of Empathy." Ohio State College of Medicine, 2023. https://medicine.osu.edu/ohio-state-medicine-dr-bradford-message/august-2023.

Blessings

Bowler, Kate, and Jessica Richie. "A Blessing for When Caring Costs You." *Good Enough: 40ish Devotions for a Life of Imperfection,* Convergent Books, 2022.

Books

Santorelli, Saki. *Heal Thy Self: Lessons on Mindfulness in Medicine.* Harmony, 2000.

Sulmasy, Daniel. *A Balm for Gilead: Meditations on Spirituality and the Healing Arts.* Georgetown University Press, 2006.

Poetry

Dickinson, Emily. "If I Can Stop One Heart from Breaking." *The Complete Poems of Emily Dickinson,* Back Bay Books, 1976.

Sacred Writing and Stories

The Bible, *Luke 10:25-37*

Kisa Gotami and the Mustard Seed, an ancient Buddhist story

My Friend Richard

In many ways, friends shape our lives, anchor us, make us feel heard and needed, make us laugh, and comfort us when we cry. Many of our friends come and go during a long lifetime, but some are there for the duration. Of all the friends we enjoy in our lives, there is something very special about that childhood friend who follows us into adulthood, who knows us inside and out, with whom we have very few secrets. It's a bond that lasts a lifetime and something we can only experience fully if it begins in our formative years.

Richard was my childhood friend. We were inseparable in school growing up, then roommates in college, growing into manhood together. When it came time for medical school, I went to Dallas, and Richard went to Houston where he would start his career. We drifted apart in those pre-cellphone years, each in a different world, each of those worlds with its own all-encompassing gravitational pull. I knew he had been depressed at times as far back as high school, but he always seemed to snap out of it.

We took a vacation together on a break that last summer and he just wasn't his old self. I couldn't quite put my finger on what had changed, but he was different. Our minds and energy were so preoccupied in that pivotal time as our careers were forming. A few months later, I got the call one evening from a mutual friend in Houston that Richard had taken his life. As I tried unsuccessfully to piece it all together in the days, then years, that followed, there were only fragmented stories of those last weeks, none fitting together. To this day, I have no idea if he made any attempt to get help or if anyone tried to help him.

In the years since we started our programs for physicians, I have seen courageous colleagues get the help they needed with counseling or a recovery program. I've seen them make life-changing course corrections: escaping a toxic work environment, cutting hours, developing healthier habits, connecting with colleagues, making a career change, reconnecting with family, or leaving direct patient care if that's what they need. Still, we find in some of our colleagues a certain sense of cynicism or anger or hopelessness, sometimes a sense of shame that prevents them from reaching out to those who could help them, often refusing help from those who offer. Still, we must try.

In a *New York Times* article, Clay Routledge writes about suicide as an existential crisis and notes that, "In order to keep existential anxiety at bay, we must find and maintain perceptions of our lives as meaningful." He goes on to say, "How do we find meaning and purpose in our lives? There are many paths, but the psychological literature suggests that close relationships with other people are our greatest existential resource."

My friend Richard may be the best friend I'll ever have. I have many happy memories of growing up together but also regrets. It is a difficult story to tell more than four decades later. I still live in the same neighborhood where we grew up and just a few blocks from the dorm and apartment we shared in college. So many things prompt fond and funny memories despite the tragic ending of his life. I will always carry his memory close to my heart, sometimes even silently speaking with him, as his presence is still so strongly felt. It taught me a lesson that is never too late to learn—that human beings have an innate, critical need to be connected with each other. We need to look out for each other. We are called to check in with colleagues, especially if you sense they are struggling, sometimes even if they resist. What you think might be an awkward conversation with a friend might just save someone's career, their marriage, perhaps even their life.

Suggested Reading

Articles

Routledge, Clay. "Suicides Have Increased. Is this an Existential Crisis?" *New York Times,* 23 June 2018. https://www.nytimes.com/2018/06/23/opinion/sunday/suicide-rate-existential-crisis.html

Blessings

O'Donohue, John. "For the Family and Friends of a Suicide." *To Bless the Space Between Us: A Book of Blessings,* Doubleday, 2008.

Poetry

Kunitz, Stanley. "The Long Boat." *Passing Through: The Later Poems, New & Selected,* Norton, 1995.

Oliver, Mary. "The Journey." *Dream Work,* Penguin, 1986.

Song Lyrics

The Fray. "How to Save a Life." *How to Save a Life,* Epic, 2005.

The 109th Bead

My colleague and mentor, Walter, died about twenty years into my career. I first met him when I was in Austin interviewing for jobs a few months before I finished my fellowship. One of the senior partners at a prestigious clinic was a family friend and asked me to come by while I was in town. I don't think they told Walt that I was going to interview, and we caught him somewhat by surprise in the hallway as he was seeing patients.

In those days, every exam room door had a plastic chart holder. As we ambushed Walt in the middle of his clinic, and he politely asked me a few questions, I leaned against a door as we chatted. Unfortunately, I leaned against a chart holder and, with a crack as loud as a gunshot, broke the thing in half. Cool and confident, I continued talking as if nothing had happened, Walt deadpanning a quizzical look. At some point I just couldn't hold it back anymore, and I started laughing hysterically. Walt didn't think it was all that funny and, in the end, my goofball interview did not end with me working there. Despite that, a few years later as a solo practitioner, Walt and I began many years of sharing calls together and as I reflected on him after his death, I realize how many things he taught me in those years, many of which I integrated into my own practice without even realizing it.

For almost twenty years, I have had the privilege of writing memorials in our county medical society magazine. The vast majority of colleagues I write about are people I have known during my thirty-five year career. Each time I sit down to write a memorial, I marvel at what they did as physicians, but also about their lives outside of medicine—rich lives previously unknown to me, even though I thought I knew many of them well. I often think of doctors who I have worked with—colleagues, mentors and teachers—many of whom are gone now but gave me gifts that I still call on today. They likely had no idea that I would see things in them that I would carry with me that make me a better doctor and a better man. It is much the same with memorable patients or their families. More times than I can count, they too have given me gifts that I call on each and every day.

When I was a senior resident on ICU rotation, one night I was checking in on a patient dying of congestive heart failure. His elderly wife was holding vigil at his bedside, all 80 pounds of her, her skin wrinkled and brown as leather from years of hard work in the New Mexico sun. She had her rosary always in hand and stood up with respect as we entered his room. In the days before laptops or cell phones, our white coats had enormous pockets, big enough to hold the spiralbound *Washington Manual*, cheat notes, "code cards," stethoscopes, and reflex hammers. These items were the paraphernalia that we thought we needed, and I suppose actually *did* need. She came close and put a tiny metal crucifix in one of my pockets without explanation. It is a great metaphor for all the wisdom that patients and colleagues have put in my pockets over the years that I carry with me, most of whom had no idea they had placed things there. With or without realizing it, I have accessed all of them through the years.

In the introduction to *Eat, Pray, Love*, Elizabeth Gilbert makes reference to the mala beads, which have been used for centuries to assist devout Hindus and Buddhists in staying focused during prayerful meditation. It is a string of 108 beads (from which the Catholic rosary was derived after the Crusades) that is held in one hand by the faithful as they meditate, their mantra repeated as they finger each bead in sequence. The mala has a special, extra bead, the 109th bead, that dangles separate from the rest like a pendant. As they reach the 109th bead, they pause and touch it, at which time they stop and thank their teachers and mentors, along with many others who have touched their lives in a lasting way.

I am writing this as I am sitting in the surgical waiting room at the teaching hospital adjacent to our medical school awaiting news from my wife's surgeons. Somewhere down the hall, two neurosurgeons who I have come to trust and admire are drawing upon their years of training, fondness for my wife, and most certainly, from the many things dropped in their pockets by patients and colleagues through the years.

Suggested Reading

Poetry

Gibran, Kahlil. "On Teaching." *The Prophet,* Knopf, 1923.

Oliver, Mary. "Thirst." *Thirst,* Beacon Press, 2007.

The Snow Storm

I was a senior medicine resident in the ICU at the VA hospital in Albuquerque one night back in the 1980s. There was a terrible sleet storm outside, the roads were impassable, and we were going to have to cover the unit for a second night. Miles away in a remote area to the north, a blizzard was in progress. Somehow, Life Flight got out ahead of the storm and transported Ray, who landed on my service. He arrived in cardiogenic shock with the ominous tall, wide ST elevations—"tombstones"—of a massive anterior myocardial infarction, signifying what in that era would likely be fatal.

The usual frenzy of activity followed, using protocols that sound primitive now, all the while knowing his chances were slim. He rallied for a while and was conversant, but seemed resigned to his fate. He reminded me of my grandfather, who was the same age and had also served in France in the First World War. He told me about his ranch, snow-covered now, but soon, in the spring, lush green pastures would re-emerge in this deep valley, snow-fed streams winding through it. It was paradise for him, sacred ground where his wife was now stranded without phone service. Tomorrow his son would have to try and drive the pickup into the pasture, and his grandson would push square bales out into the snow for the hungry cattle. The old man's face was pale, deeply creased, sun-damaged, at times welling up with tears. Things were quiet for a while, and I sat with him, and he became unresponsive.

In a long career it's surprising how certain patients, even from the distant past, can stick in your mind. I remember those hours vividly, watching life slowly ebb from him as his heart failed, checking on him almost constantly, sitting by his bed, drawn to him, considering the heart. Not just the pump, but his *spiritual heart* and what might become of that when the physical one stopped.

Virtually every major religion and non-religious spiritual discipline attach special, sacred significance to the heart. References to this are even found in ancient Egyptian art, in ancient mythology, in timeless Native American lore and art. The heart is a transformative symbol connecting humans, nature, and the spirit world. It is often seen as a place where the soul resides, the center of emotions and morals, compassion and courage, wisdom and peace, and the source of love. It is a place where we might encounter inner peace, even sense the presence of the transcendent. We tend to go to great lengths on outward journeys throughout life looking for wisdom and peace and love in the world around us, but the real work takes place when we go inward, into the heart.

Occasionally, medicine calls on us to share our heart with a patient in need. Daniel Sulmasy notes that, "If we are committed to healing patients as whole persons, we must understand not only what disease and injury do to their bodies, but what disease and injury do to them as embodied spiritual persons ... Illness raises troubling questions of a transcendent nature—questions about meaning, value, and relationship. These are spiritual questions. How we answer these questions *for ourselves* will affect the ways we help our patients struggle with these questions." Ultimately, our inner journey to wholeness is for those around us as much as it is for us. Ethicist Paul Ramsey describes us as "a covenant people on a common pilgrimage." When we enter into relationship with our patients, such a covenant requires that we visibly express fidelity, love, compassion, and justice—acknowledgment of the sanctity of life—as we honor that relationship.

In those hours, I felt about as close to Ray as you can with a patient, but I did not have what I sensed he needed from me. I was able to listen, to touch his shoulder, to hear his stories, and that mattered, but I was young and had not experienced enough of life or my own inner journey to be able to help him deeply in those last hours. Generous listening, presence, comforting with touch. Yes, touch. In this moment, touch seemed so important. It sounds so simple, so basic, but in that moment, it was more important than anything else I had to offer. The time for medical heroics had passed. This was the time for shared humanity. It isn't something taught in medical school . . . because it can't be taught. It must be discovered. Only its importance can be taught. At the time, and for all these years after, I remember vividly those hours and feel I helped him in his transition.

Later in life as I remember it, I now see it was a privilege, a gift he gave to me, to have accompanied him on the last part of his journey with my presence in those hours, a great gift that night that helped me with other patients in the years that followed.

Ray never woke up—he died just before rounds the next morning. There was someone in his little cubicle almost every minute since his arrival but sure enough, the minute he was alone he passed away. We were just a few feet away gathering for rounds, talking about the storm. I tried his home number again and this time his wife answered. I tried to convey how he described his love of his family and the land, but I don't think she heard anything after the first sentence. By late afternoon, the roads were passable and I went home. And slept.

Suggested Reading

Books

Kane, Jeff. *The Healing Companion: Simple and Effective Ways Your Presence Can Help People Heal.* HarperSanFrancisco, 2001.

Ramsey, Paul. *The Patient as Person: Explorations in Medical Ethics*. Yale University Press, 1970.

Sulmasy, Daniel. *A Balm for Gilead: Meditations on Spirituality and the Healing Arts*. Georgetown University Press, 2006.

Poetry

Rumi. "Passion." *Rumi: Passion for the Divine*, translated by Shahram Shiva, Hohm Press, 2003.

TURNING INTO THE STORM

Turning into the Storm

I had a conversation recently with a retired naval officer who did several tours on aircraft carriers years ago. Somehow the conversation turned to storms at sea and how crews prepare a carrier to meet them. Storms are not always avoidable and sometimes taking refuge in a harbor is riskier than being on the open sea. The captain of the ship and his crew must be ready to act long before a storm hits. This readiness involves practice, skill, and leadership. In addition to the work of the crew, part of the preparation lies in the construction of the carrier itself. The front, or bow, of the ship has a highly reinforced frame. On the open sea, captains endeavor to turn the carrier directly into the storm, as the bow is constructed to withstand the assault better than the sides, which will protect crew and cargo. Although most ships of that size are usually safer at sea than in a harbor during a storm, sometimes they take shelter in protected areas away from open sea, where they often depend on their massive anchor systems. This naval officer served on older carriers, where anchors weigh 60,000 pounds and are connected by up to a quarter mile of chain, each link weighing around 150 pounds. Anchors are important, but as I thought about it, so too is the courage it takes for the captain to turn the ship and its crew directly into potentially catastrophic storms.

    I've spent very little time in my life on a boat any bigger than a bass boat, but I'm still a sucker for nautical metaphors and it struck me as we were speaking that there are similarities between what he described and our lives in medicine. Specifically, day-to-day practice is hard enough, but predictably we all face times of crisis caring for patients, navigating our practice environments, or dealing with personal matters. As David Whyte describes it, our times of crisis can be like "the meeting of two immense storm fronts, the squally vulnerable edge between what overwhelms human beings from the inside and what overpowers them from the outside."

During years of spending time with physicians in our counseling and recovery programs, it's become clear that without certain anchors in place, without honoring and nurturing them, without preparing ourselves for turbulence in life, we are set adrift and become vulnerable to the inevitable storms of life. How well we weather these storms depends on how we prepare ourselves as we go through our days and how we equip ourselves with a strong mindset and inner resources. This is what anchors us through good times and bad. We weather life's storms with courage, faith, values, a sense of calling, patience, and importantly, with love. These storms lead us to discovery, where we become more discerning and learn how to heal the world around us without making the storms a permanent part of our daily lives.

For a few years early in my career, not by coincidence, I practiced just a few doors down the hall from my father-in-law. I started dating his daughter when we were still in middle school, and he was like a father to me. At a certain point late in his career, his wife (my mother-in-law) was in the final stages of dying from metastatic lung cancer, which was a difficult, lingering journey for all of us. That same year, he had quite unfairly been named in a very nasty malpractice suit. One day as I was rounding next door at the hospital, I could hear him speaking with a patient and I stopped to listen. It turned out that she too was in the last stages of cancer. I couldn't hear all that was said, but at one point I heard him tell her, "Yes, terrible, unfair things happen to us in this life and I'm sorry you are going through this, but your family loves you and we love you. We will be right here with you and take good care of you." The door was half open and I could see his back as he sat in a chair pulled up close to her bed. The room became very quiet. I saw a couple of patients and a half hour later when I passed the room again, he was still sitting there with her, both of them in silence. I will always remember that moment, that man who taught me so much, illustrating most of the qualities that define a good doctor and a good man. A man who was no stranger to storms and was not afraid to turn into them head on.

Suggested Reading

Books

Whyte, David. "Crisis." *Consolations: The Solace, Nourishment and Underlying Meaning of Everyday Words,* Many Rivers Press, 2021.

Poetry

Thakkar, Aashka. "Confide in a Friend." *PoemHunter*, 2009.

Scripture

The Bible, *Mark 4:35-41*

The Bible, *Deuteronomy 31:6*

Calling

We all sense that we are here for a purpose, that somehow we fit into the fabric of life in some important way, that we have something to give to the world. One reason doctors so often struggle in our professional lives these days is that when others control how we practice, the character and priorities in our work shift. Supreme importance is shifted to income produced ("production numbers"), as if we are churning out widgets. Non-clinical administrative burdens are off loaded to us, filling our days (and nights) with meaningless tasks. The result is that our daily work often cannot honor our calling, or worse, it is in conflict with it. A sense of calling is a basic human need; translating that into visible work (vocation) is fundamental to a life of meaning and contentment. Without realizing it, or worse, recognizing it and ignoring it, we are set adrift lost in day-to-day routines that are ultimately unfulfilling.

For simplicity, let's define "a job" as how we make a living and "a career" as dedicated work that offers opportunities for growth, stability, and pride. Calling and vocation may or may not be part of either of these, even for a physician. In fact, sometimes the job we find ourselves in can sometimes work to separate us from our calling. Parker Palmer explains, "We arrive in this world with birthright gifts—then spend the first half of our lives abandoning them or letting others disabuse us of them. Our original shape is deformed beyond recognition; and we ourselves, driven by fear, too often betray our true self to gain the approval of others."

Finding our calling involves discerning our unique gifts and passions, as well as our own vision of what the people and world around us cry out for. For some, calling and vocation aren't fully realized in our workday, perhaps by the nature of our practice situation or because our unique calling involves something beyond our work in medicine. If so, then our lives beyond the boundaries of our job must express our calling to fully realize what we are meant to be in this world.

The process of discovering our calling is not easy and is never fully completed. It is the work of a lifetime, as our calling may change as we go through different seasons of our life. The realization of our calling is ultimately our search for meaning and wholeness. Joan Chittister sums it up well in *Let Your Life Speak,* noting that achieving a life of wholeness, "is a matter of listening to the call—to the magnet of the heart within us—to assess our own gifts, to follow our own passions, and to find, through them, the happiness that flows from the fit between passion and purpose . . ." Even if we are fortunate enough to discern a clear sense of vocational calling, we must not let that displace our most essential callings: to cherish and nurture our families, to support and celebrate our friends, to embrace, honor, and have faith in transcendent truths.

In recent years, two friends of mine have exhibited a sense of calling in its purest form. One was a fine acute care doctor, a kind, sensitive, loving, and creative soul. In mid-career and with a family to provide for, they stepped away from work that was causing distress. This work no longer nourished them, so they made a career change to palliative care, a specialty to which I believe they are ideally suited and will do great good in. It involved a mid-career reentry into a training program, something that surely was not easy for them or their family. Another friend is a talented pediatrician who also walked away from a full practice to build, from scratch, a non-profit serving children of undocumented immigrants who have limited resources for healthcare in our community. It was an act of love and sacrifice—an act of following a calling which to that point had not been fully answered. Answering our calling is a visible way of sharing our gifts and what lies deep within our hearts.

Not everyone who goes into medicine does so with a clear sense of altruistic calling, and many who once felt this calling abandon it when faced with the complexities of life and the business of medicine. Even if our calling is closely aligned with our work as physicians, we must also undertake the often difficult task of making sure that where, how, and with whom we undertake that work honors and encourages that sense of calling. This is a task that can require the courage of our convictions when it is at odds with practice leadership or corporate structure. Working in an environment that does not allow us to reach the full potential of our calling is the surest way to spend our days in frustration, even despair. It sometimes forces us to make the hard decision to confront a system and the people leading it who ignore our calling and values. It sometimes requires us to walk away from a job that fails to nourish us, in search of something better before it's too late.

Suggested Reading

Books

Chittister, Joan. *Following the Path: The Search for a Life of Passion, Purpose, and Joy.* Image,

2012.

Palmer, Parker J. *Let Your Life Speak: Listening for the Voice of Vocation.* Jossey-Bass, 1999.

Poetry

Frost, Robert. "The Road Not Taken." *Mountain Interval.* Henry Holt and Company, 1916.

Scripture

The Bible, *2 Peter 1:10*

The Bible, *Ephesians 4:1-2*

Faith

It's funny how there are people, places, and things in our lives that we encounter repeatedly, sometimes for decades, without noticing them until one day they change our lives forever.

For the first twenty years of my medical practice, most days I drove to a hospital a couple of miles away to make rounds. Each time, I would drive by an Episcopal Seminary, an imposing, historic mansion surrounded by modern classroom and office buildings. At a low point with my wife's medical struggles, burnout at work, and typical unanswered midlife existential questions, I impulsively turned into the campus one day and went, unannounced, into the admissions office.

For the next five years, I took almost every class available to me, eventually being told I was eligible for a couple of degrees and my time there was done—something that did not come as good news. Those were great years. I met all kinds of people with diverse backgrounds, personal histories, and spiritual beliefs who changed my life. There were many questions I had when I started my studies, almost none of which were answered in those years. I learned a lot of theology and church history, but much of the mystery of life's ultimate meaning remained elusive, and so did faith at times. Scripture tells us, "Now faith is the assurance of things hoped for, the conviction of things unseen." I now fully understand and appreciate that verse in ways that are strangely comforting. Faith, we are also told in scripture, is a gift; it is ours for the taking, if we will only do so. I left seminary with a degree in pastoral ministry. That seemed more appropriate than a divinity degree for someone with so many doubts.

What I really learned in those years is that doubt is okay. Mystery is okay and so is admitting that questions of faith and meaning will always elude us, even if our faith is strong, but especially when it wavers. Those years gave me freedom, curiosity, and the language to openly discuss these things, to engage others, to share my faith journey with them.

Research shows that the overwhelming percentage of our patients wish we would discuss spirituality with them, but that only a tiny fraction of us do. I'm not talking about proselytizing. I'm not talking about unsolicited stories of my personal beliefs about God or my doubts. Neither am I saying they are anything to hide if asked. Spirituality takes as many forms as there are people, but there are transcendent questions that many of our patients wish we would be open to having a dialogue about—even if it's just generous listening—and ignoring this need leaves out an important component of holistic care for our patients and perhaps some deep sense of meaning and connection for us in our own work.

So why do we ignore the spiritual needs of our patients? Research suggests that for most, it's an issue of time and volume in our strange world of RVU (Relative Value Unit) driven medical care, where physicians' value to their practice is quantified using monetary metrics, rather than by the more intangible sense of caring that patients desire. For others, there is discomfort in mixing science with spirituality. Some don't feel properly equipped or trained for such a discussion. Others feel their own spirituality—or lack thereof—is too personal to risk sharing. And as we all know, but hate to admit, some of our colleagues just can't be bothered.

While it wouldn't be expected to have this kind of discourse with all, or even most, patients, it's much needed by many patients facing life-altering, chronic diseases and end-of-life care. They may or may not ask for us to address their spiritual needs or faith, but it's part of our calling to gently approach it. It's about them, not about us, but a certain healing for both physician and patient often occurs when such a relationship develops. In those situations, we hope that our honest dialogue and generous listening with our patient is both comforting and therapeutic for them, but so often in that setting, it is therapeutic for us as well.

In the early '90s, a beloved and memorable patient of mine developed severe arthritis. She was in her late thirties, whip smart, and experiencing a meteoric rise in a high profile career. She was married and had an entertaining, precocious young child whom she occasionally brought along with her to office visits. She developed rheumatoid arthritis just three or four years before our breakthrough biologic modifying treatments became available. Her disease was so severe the first couple of years that she had to step away from her work and hire a nanny to help her with basic care of her child. I only saw her spouse once; the sudden change in their lives dealt a fatal blow to their marriage within a couple of years. Although she was a woman of faith, the sudden severity of her illness that robbed her of so much triggered a crisis of faith, and she abandoned it. It was not just a crisis in her religious faith, but also a crisis of faith in herself, in her ability to take on the world with both hands, to raise a confident child, and to be strong in her marriage. In those days when our treatments for rheumatoid disease were often lacking, her story was not unusual. She and I were not too far apart in age, but I was young in my career and was not confident in initiating conversations that offered patients a way to address their spiritual needs.

One day quite out of the blue, she asked me about my religious background. We had a long conversation about faith, both in a religious context and also in a more generic, but deeply spiritual context. We discussed how severe illness often shakes our very foundations; it can make us question everything about ourselves and God. It created a closeness between us and gave her an outlet to discuss how the illness had affected her entire life, a conversation that I gathered she couldn't bring herself to have with friends or family. That conversation, and those that followed, had a visible therapeutic effect on her, likely more than some of the treatments I prescribed. That experience forever changed the way I thought about conversations with patients and the yearning that many of them have to discuss spiritual issues.

By the late 1990s, biologic modifying therapy became widely available, and while some damage had been done, she had a near miraculous response to treatment. She was able to resume her career and eventually found a new life partner before moving away. The mystery—the miracle—of her life changing response to newly available treatment was not lost on her and her gratitude fueled her rediscovered faith. In many ways her faith was restored, perhaps tempered by the intense fire of life-changing illness and her determination to live life to the fullest. Like her, my own faith has wavered many times, and like her, there have been people in my life who have helped me through those times.

For me, listening to my patients about spirituality and faith, encouraging that dialogue when appropriate and desired, was a skill that did not come naturally. Turning into the seminary campus that day was life changing, though I'm the first to admit that it's not for everyone. I have a long way to go, but on a good day, I think I can say those years changed the way I interact with the world around me. They grounded me and gave me a new way to more gently interact with my patients. My faith still wavers frequently, but the mystery of that no longer worries me or makes me feel that I have failed in some way. Most days now I have a pretty good sense of what lies within my heart, and a pretty good idea about how to connect with it . . . if I only try.

Suggested Reading

Articles

Sulmasy, Daniel. "Is Medicine a Spiritual Practice?" *Academy of Medicine,* vol. 74, no. 9, 1999. https://pubmed.ncbi.nlm.nih.gov/10498092/.

Books

Santorelli, Saki. *Heal Thyself: Lessons on Mindfulness in Medicine.* Harmony, 2000.

Poetry

Oliver, Mary. "Praying." *Thirst,* Beacon Press, 2007.

Scripture

The Bible, *Hebrews 11:1*
The Bible, *Matthew 28:16-20*

Love

It's surprising how little is written about love in physician wellness literature. Defining love is hard. Just try. However you define it, I doubt that your words come anywhere near a satisfactory description. Part of the problem is that there are so many kinds of love. Philosophers of antiquity described distinct types of love: *eros, philia, storge, agape, platonic*. Ultimately, it is foundational in our lives and yet hard to express in words—but we know it when we feel it.

Perhaps love in the sense that I'm using here is the kind of love that is universal and unconditional—the hardest of all to define, describe or even comprehend fully. This ultimate kind of love connects us with each other and with the universe or higher powers beyond ourselves—concepts which we can scarcely pretend to understand. This kind of love is messy, and it calls us to share love equally with all those around us, even those who are seemingly unlovable.

Decades later, I remember how an attending pointed this out to me when I was an intern. We saw a patient on rounds who was in police custody, restrained, and in the throes of withdrawal. The room was full of the overwhelming and unmistakable smell of steatorrhea. The squirming, delirious man was suffering greatly. The patient we had seen immediately before him, Mrs. Turner I'll call her, was a delightful, entertaining elderly woman who we had all come to love in the week she had spent with us. Out in the hallway, our attending who was the department chair, commented, "The most important thing to learn today is that we have to care for, and about, this man just as we do for Mrs. Turner."

When you try to remember why you went into medicine, some of you might remember that it was an interest in science, a doctor you admired growing up, the concept of being wealthy and without a boss, or any number of other reasons. However, I can assure you that for virtually all of you, the real reason you spent your youth studying all those hours, being on call, missing sleep, getting frustrated and exhausted was love. Love makes all of that, then and now, worthwhile. Love propels you into the next exam room or operating room or to carefully examine the next scan or slide. It fills in the gaps where science leaves off. Love, not RVUs, a brilliant diagnosis, or the perfect EMR note, is the source of healing for your patient and for you.

One night almost exactly twenty-nine years ago, I sat with the MRI tech at Seton and looked at images of my wife's lumbar spine as they came up. A neuroradiologist acquaintance looked at the images with me. Tumor filled the spinal canal, it wrapped around and compressed the spinal cord and caudal nerves. I didn't know exactly what I was looking at, but I knew it was bad. I don't remember what my colleague said, but I do remember he put his hand on my shoulder. I still remember that simple act that was a pure and spontaneous expression of love given by a relative stranger on that awful night that made me feel less alone.

There is an unwavering, unending love that is around us and within us as we move through our days caring for patients and colleagues. Our job is to stay connected to it—to ponder it, embrace it, and share it. As you pause at the doorway to the next patient, don't just take a breath, take a breath and think... "love." It may conjure up love for the patient waiting to see you, love for the work you do, or for life in general, but whatever it connects you with, it will make the next few minutes something that it might not have otherwise been for either one of you.

Suggested Reading

Poetry

Kaur, Rupi. "most importantly love." *milk and honey,* Andrews McMeel Publishing, 2015.

Oliver, Mary. "Don't Hesitate." *Swan,* Beacon Press, 2012.

Scripture

The Bible, *I Corinthians 13:4-8*

Courage

There are many terrible ways to die, and ALS must be near the top of that list. A steady downhill progression of losing function and independence with a sad, predictable end. I've always been in awe of families and patients who go down that long road. A decade ago, a longtime colleague wrote an essay to be distributed throughout our physician wellness program telling the story of his journey with ALS as he neared the end. He laboriously wrote it with an eye movement guided computer program, as he was fully immobile and required ventilator support. It was hard to read and provoked many emotions—sadness to be sure—but it was also a story of great courage and acceptance that was inspiring, of a fine man who squeezed every morsel out of life to the very end.

Looking for examples of courage to write about, I reread it again recently. As it happened, as I reread it I had been with two longtime friends who were both fighting advanced, likely terminal cancer against great odds. Each friend was going through the two-front battle of resistance and acceptance, each of which is needed when faced with serious health problems. Their courage has made me reconsider bravery in all the ways that we see it and what an admirable quality it is. It also occurred to me that often there is courage that is less grand, often hidden, yet there nonetheless, and how in many ways it takes courage—daily courage—to practice medicine.

The kind of courage we usually think about involves soldiers or first responders. Courage that involves protesting injustice or discrimination or calling out those in power who misuse it. Courage that goes into danger to help the poor, the hungry, or those with no voice. Courage that not too long ago we saw in our colleagues on the front lines facing a deadly pandemic. This is obvious courage. But far more commonly, there is a silent, hidden kind of courage that each and every one of you exhibits, most likely in ways that even you are not aware.

Each of us has things that are particularly challenging for us in our daily work. For me, in my work, particularly early in my career, it's always been confronting contentious, angry patients with news they don't want to hear. It's hard to discuss a treatment that failed or caused complications, or point out lifestyle or medical decisions they made that harmed their health. I'm non-confrontational by nature. Standing up to angry, sometimes even verbally abusive patients has always caused me to have to dig deep and find the courage to show confidence I'm not always feeling, to push back where needed for their own good. At a handful of crossroads in my career, it's taken courage to change my practice setting, to end or start partnerships with the many unknowns that go with that.

There is great courage in caring for patients, in opening every exam room door, every operating room door. Courage in caring for people with complex diseases when the risks are high and the outcome far from certain. Courage even in the most casual, seemingly simple medical encounters where we all know things can unexpectedly go terribly wrong. It is a kind of courage that is just assumed we carry with us, and carry it we must, even when it often goes hand-in-hand with self-doubt or even fear. Even the most courageous should admit to fear as they face it down. Brené Brown calls on us to redefine courage, noting that, "Vulnerability is our most accurate measure of courage . . . it is willingness to show up and be seen when you can't control the outcome or what other people think."

We don't leave courage at the door when we go home at night. Few things require more courage than parenting, where the stakes are high, and too often uncertainty exceeds even that which we experience at work. Uncertainty about how we parent. Uncertainty about seemingly insignificant actions, which can intentionally or unintentionally change the trajectory of our children's lives, for better or worse, in ways only seen and realized years later when they are fully formed adults. There is courage in long-term relationships, in being seen and loved then giving it back through the years, in seeing loved ones not just in joy but also through life's inevitable struggles. Courage is most often our extraordinary response to ordinary things we encounter throughout our lives. Sometimes only in retrospect can we see that actions were heroic, when they just seemed to be a reflexive response at the time. Sometimes courage is demonstrated not in a single act, but rather over a very long period of time.

Yes, I have greatly admired the courage I have seen in my dear friends facing mortal challenges recently, and I'm inspired by it, but I am also inspired by less conspicuous acts of courage that I am coming to realize surround me as I go through my days at work and with my family. Courage is not the absence of fear; it is perseverance, even passion, in the face of it. Look around at the fearless way you and your colleagues go through your days, even when there is doubt, and all the good you bring into the world as you do it. Appreciate it for what it is. Courage is inspired by, fueled by, made fearless by our love for the people and calling we hold in our hearts, for the love of life itself.

Suggested Reading

Books

Brown, Brené. *The Power of Vulnerability: Teachings of Authenticity, Connection, and Courage.* Sounds True, 2012. Audiobook.

Poetry

Sexton, Anne. "Courage." *The Awful Rowing Toward God*, Houghton Mifflin, 1975.

SCENERY

The Acorn

A year into the pandemic, stir crazy and probably not thinking straight, I bought a fifteen acre olive grove near La Grange. Just before we bought it, it had two hundred mature olive trees, a restored farmhouse, one hundred-sixty-year-old log cabin and, to me at least, the place seemed magical. Of course, there is a reason why Texas is not known for its olive industry, and that terrible freeze in 2021 killed off the entire orchard. In the years that followed, I've planted all kinds of trees in the groves—apples, plums, and pears—and only a dozen or so apple trees have survived the droughts and heat.

As I sat on the front porch of the house one breezy, quiet Saturday early last spring, the struggling fruit trees in the distance taunting me, I realized I was looking at what just might be the perfect tree. Tall, perfectly round, and deep green, it stands at the center of the property, and is an example of nature's perfection for which I can claim no credit. Somehow, I had not really noticed it before. It sounds silly, but that day a certain kind of wisdom about the land came to me: to watch and listen to the land, to learn its secrets, to honor and enjoy it rather than try to make it something it cannot be. It seems so obvious now. It's not that it's "not nice to fool Mother Nature" as the commercial from a few years ago said. It's that trying to fool Mother Nature is . . . well, just a fool's errand.

Life is full of mystery. In my work in medicine, I often come up against diagnostic dilemmas. Years ago, I learned that what some of my patients suffer from defies understanding in its earliest presentations, no matter how hard I try to figure it out. The process sometimes must unfold over months or years before we are sure about it, something I've come to terms with, but something understandably so hard for most patients to accept.

A mentor early in my career told a story from a national meeting where the speaker, describing a particularly vexing case, famously said, "Having failed to make a diagnosis, we proceeded with treatment."

The story sounded ridiculous at the time, but now I think I understand what he was trying to say. Even as some conditions very slowly unfold, we must still be present and engaged with the patient, all the while trying to share with them an understanding that mystery is always part of life and frequently part of medical care. Honoring that, being honest and humble about it, all the while holding our patient's hand is sometimes what is called for and is one of the most difficult things we do.

Accepting mystery, observing the world with curiosity, and patiently letting life unfold is how we acquire wisdom. Accepting mystery is not easy. It requires patience and an open heart in a world that more often wants to harden our hearts. Physician wellness pioneer Rachel Naomi Remen writes of the "buddha seed" in all of us waiting to become a tree of wisdom if we will only allow it. She said, "Life offers its wisdom generously. Everything teaches. Life asks us the same thing we have been asked in every class: 'Stay awake.' 'Pay attention.' Wisdom comes most easily to those who have the courage to embrace life without judgment and are willing to *not know*, sometimes for a long time . . . It involves a change in our basic nature, a deepening of our capacity for compassion, loving-kindness, forgiveness, harmlessness, and service. Life waters the buddha seed within us."

Mystery is often a prelude to miracles. Within every acorn, there is a yearning and the mysterious possibility of becoming a beautiful oak tree. Clueless for so long about this land, and now at least a little wiser and more observant through painful failure, I've started planting live oak trees around our little "Grove House," the house's name now relegated to quotation marks. A couple of years in, they are growing nicely, but slowly—as oak trees do. By the end of this year, I will have planted one for each of our eight grandchildren, and ultimately, the planting is not for me. Like my grandchildren, these trees will reach maturity in an unseen future many years from now. As I sit on the front porch on this magnificent spring morning, studying nature's perfect tree and the much younger trees planted nearby, I smile to think that one day each of my grandchildren might sit in the shade of these very trees.

Suggested Reading

Books

Gibran, Kahlil. "On Children." *The Prophet,* Knopf, 1923.

Remen, Rachel Naomi. *My Grandfather's Blessings: Stories of Strength, Refuge and Belonging.* Riverhead Books, 2001.

Poetry

Oliver, Mary. "Morning Poem." *Dream Work,* Penguin, 1986.

Oliver, Mary. "Mystery, Yes." *Why I Wake Early,* Beacon Press, 2004.

Let It Be

While driving to our weekend property out in the cattle country of central Texas recently, I listened to a podcast with Paul McCartney detailing the backstory behind the greatest hits of the Beatles and his own solo career. He was telling the story of "Let It Be," a song he wrote as it became clear the Beatles would break up, with all the anger and angst that would bring. He recalls that one night amid all that stress and conflict he had a dream. In it, his mother, Mary, who died when he was an adolescent, came to him and consoled him. She guided him to acceptance and peace, in essence . . . to let it be. In a time of turmoil, the resulting song and its meaning became a great comfort to him, an anthem of sorts for the band, and a message of peace for the millions of listeners in the next half century and beyond.

Later in the interview, it came to him that

perhaps another origin of the song may have come from studying *Hamlet* in high school. We all remember the "to be or not to be . . ." soliloquy, but almost no one remembers that later in the play, when his fate is sealed, acceptance emerges. Hamlet answers his own question twice, once nearing death when he tells Horatio, "Had I but time . . . oh, I could tell you . . . But let it be." Well, clearly McCartney remembers Hamlet better than I do—apparently, I had my mind on other things in high school—but Shakespeare's point is made along with countless songwriters and poets, saints and prophets. Acceptance is a pathway to peace.

After a long day working and clearing my head around the property, in the early evening I sat down as a few swallows made their final flights. Sitting near my fledgling apple grove and the pond with its large turtles still moving about, I was at peace. Nature is the great salve; sitting in the gloaming my mind wandered where it will, but mostly I observed creation. The neighbor was cutting hay earlier, partly interrupted by a brief shower, and the fragrance of wet hay lingered. With the creeping darkness, the songbirds were silenced. All the sounds—tractors, cattle trailers rattling down the narrow county road, the occasional faraway whine of a chainsaw—disappeared, and there was quiet. Gradually it was replaced by the croaking of frogs, all manner of insect noises and more—all the sounds of the night that a city boy can neither identify nor be entirely comfortable with.

I have been blessed beyond measure in my life, but lately there have been worries: about a good friend, about work, about the health of some people I love, about a season of change. With some effort, it's set aside—even if just for a few breaths at a time—and replaced with acceptance and gratitude and faith. Having worries is inevitable. Living with patience, kindness, and joy in the face of it is one of the great challenges of human existence.

The world was coming to rest, even as nocturnal creatures began to prowl, unseen. But high above the cabin, above the pond and the fire, there was a crescent moon rising and countless stars with their timeless stories, and it was time to sleep. Soon enough we will rise again and there will be challenge, sometimes even tragedy, but most certainly there will be joy and beauty. Like lamenters in the Psalms, I may shake my fist at times, but always, always I will be in love.

Let it be.

Suggested Reading

Poetry

Bourdillon, Francis William. "Night." *Among the Flowers, and Other Poems,* Marcus Ward & Co, 1878.

O'Donohue, John. "Vespers." *To Bless the Space Between Us: A Book of Blessings,* Doubleday, 2008.

Oliver, Mary. "In Blackwater Woods." *American Primitive,* Back Bay Books, 1983.

Teasdale, Sara. "Twilight." *Poetry,* edited by Harriet Monroe, 1924.

Wordsworth, William. "The Stars are Mansions Built By Nature's Hand." *The Poetical Works Of*

William Wordsworth, Vol. 1, The Echo Library, 1869.

Scripture

The Bible, *John 14:27*

The Bible, *Matthew 6:34*

The Bible, *Philippians 4:6*

Song Lyrics

The Beatles. "Let It Be." *Let It Be*, Apple Records, 1970.

The Bear

In an episode of the TV show *Lucky Hank*, Hank and his wife are entertaining his not-so-beloved academic coworkers. The conversation is degenerating and to change the tone of the conversation, Hank's wife suggests a table game. She asks each person to give their two "happiness numbers": the first one being their "percent happiness" in their current life, the second number asking how low that happiness number would have to get before they would make real change in their lives. The game was a terrible idea for a party, but it made me think: during the COVID-19 pandemic, our lives turned upside down. The threshold for change for many of us had changed, often, but not always, for the better.

We saw many versions of change around us, and you may have gone through some version of the process yourself those strange days. Many of those transitions were admirable and involved careful discernment and often no small amount of sacrifice and courage. Frequent examples include: reimagining work and changing an unhappy practice situation or career direction; taking a sabbatical from practice to catch your breath; cutting back days or hours to be more present with family; shedding a bad habit or relationship.

For many people, there were other changes: pandemic pets, early retirement, the greener pastures of a vacation home or the decision to move far away. Many, if not most, of those changes share something in common—leaving something that makes us sad, anxious, or unfulfilled in search of something better. Like some of you, over the years I have made my share of missteps in seeking change. But in the moment, in real time, how do we tell the difference between necessary change and just running away? We are, after all, hardwired to run away from things that threaten us.

In his cautionary essay, "Wherever You Go, There You Are," Jon Kabat-Zinn explores the human tendency to run away. He writes, "The romantic notion is that if it's no good over here, you only have to go over there and things will be different . . . Change the location, change the circumstances, and everything will fall into place; you can start over and have a new beginning." But he points out, "You cannot escape yourself, try as you might." He calls on us to consider that true change comes from the inside rather than the outside, even when it is easier to run. Sometimes that means standing our ground.

David Whyte describes it in another way. He writes, "Wanting to run is necessary, actual running can save our lives at crucial times but can also be extremely dangerous and unwise, especially in the presence of animals that are bigger, faster, and more agile . . . In the wild, the best response to dangerous circumstances is often not to run but to assume a profoundly attentive identity, to pay attention . . . and not to assume the identity of victim." Standing our ground, confronting perceived threats, resisting the urge to flee—all of these are sometimes the hardest work we face as adults. But when it is time to run, the key, I think, is to make sure that we are running *toward* something and not just *away* from something.

Restless in that first year after the shutdown, I found myself in Colorado for a few days of hiking, hoping in vain to briefly forget the pandemic. One gorgeous fall afternoon, I was a few miles from the trailhead, when I came around a bend and found myself not more than twenty feet from a black bear. Both of us froze. I tried immediately to recall the recommended response to this situation, and based on that highly-flawed recollection, I stood very still, made eye contact with the bear and . . . sang. Somehow, I thought I was supposed to talk or quietly sing. Where I got that notion, I have no idea. I couldn't get the Bob Dylan song "Don't Think Twice, It's All Right" out of my head that day, so I quietly sang to the bear . . . or maybe to myself. The bear stared at me for a solid minute, then turned and trotted off.

Perhaps the defining moments in our lives are when we make a stand and when we run. Admittedly, it was more paralysis than bravery, but in that moment, I was just fed up enough with bears and pandemics that I refused to run away. I continued down the trail, even with the sure knowledge that there are more bears out there.

Suggested Reading

Books

Kabat-Zinn, Jon. *Wherever You Go, There You Are: Mindfulness Meditation in Everyday Life.* Hyperion, 1994.

Whyte, David. "Run Away." *Consolations: The Solace, Nourishment and Underlying Meaning of Everyday Words*, Many Rivers Press, 2021.

COMPANIONS ON THE TRAIL

The Dump Truck

I have inhabited hospitals my entire adult life professionally and yet ironically one of the most challenging things I've encountered is sitting in a hospital room with a loved one. My wife and I have been in and out of the hospital more than two dozen times in the last few years, and with each one it gets harder and harder for me. It's a complete loss of control in an environment where I used to be able to pretend I had a little bit of control as a physician. It's hard to watch someone you love suffer, and if I'm honest, it's . . . really boring. It's sort of like the opposite of dog years. Instead of time being accelerated, it comes to a crawl, at times seemingly to a complete stop, at least relative to the speed my mind is still racing. And so, I've been thinking about patience lately.

Patience is usually defined as the ability to tolerate delay, inconvenience, suffering, or habits or behavior different from your established preferences. It is the ability to tolerate things generally moving in slow motion without getting angry or upset. In a more basic sense, it is a reminder of, and rebellion against, the loss of control. It often stems from unrealistic expectations and lack of acceptance. Patience has three different domains: patience for life circumstances and hardships, patience for challenges and disappointment in relationships, and patience for the countless trivial hassles of daily life. Studies teach us that lack of patience has measurable consequences to our mental and physical health. One study even demonstrated a link between impatience and telomere shortening, a key pathway to more rapid aging.

The world that we inhabit does not encourage patience-quite the opposite. When you think about it, almost everything around us is designed for efficiency and speed. There aren't enough hours in the day for us to do what we need to do. Being trapped in a line, waiting for test results or a patient to be ready in the OR, or waiting for a child to finish eating breakfast before school—these are sudden reminders that we are not in control. When our days are consumed by the quest for speed, efficiency, and predictability needed to keep up with our own expectations, we may find ourselves speeding by people around us who are moving slower, similar to speeding past a car driving in the slow lane of a highway. We leave these people and those moments in our dust, often never to be fully connected again.

There are many techniques for cultivating patience, but they share several basic things in common. In general, these techniques may be divided into managing acute situations of impatience and more long-term strategies to develop a more patient mindset. Most of all, even the most basic mindfulness techniques can be helpful. Specifically, when you feel yourself getting impatient, simply stopping and realizing that you are being impatient-naming it-to some extent neutralizes it, but also reminds you to follow practices that help you through those moments.

Breathing exercises are an essential ingredient to both acute and long-term patience. Breathing can be performed as an independent practice or as an integral component of meditation, yoga, and other practices. Either way, it is a frequently overlooked strategy toward mental and physical health.

Breathwork has been used through the centuries, and its power has been defined in scientific studies more recently. Cultivating practices like yoga, meditation, journaling, prayer, and other techniques is highly individual and requires a certain discipline that most of us lack, but each is a clear pathway to strengthen our patience. Each in their own way has the potential as a pathway to patience, and in doing so, being able to slow down and become more aware of the gifts that are all around us.

When my two-year-old grandson River comes for a visit, with just some eye contact and pointing, we immediately embark on a routine that he will not allow us to ignore. We first go to the vast empty nesters' wasteland that is the upstairs of our home, where quite instinctively he goes to the long-abandoned bedroom of his mother. There we line up matchbox cars for a while, then open one of the windows (don't tell his mother), and, holding him tightly, we look out and watch the birds fly by and the cars or walkers pass by. I think he could do this for hours. Our next stop is the far corner of our family room where there's an antique wooden box, originally built to hold firewood. He directs me to sit in a tiny toddler's chair just inches away while one by one, he pulls out dump trucks, cars, nerf balls, Barbies, and other assorted toys one at a time, showing me each before he deposits them in a rarely-used brass trash can just a few steps away.

One by one, he does this for the twenty or thirty toys that inhabit that box, then once finished, he waits for me to tell him to move the things back to the box. The whole process takes thirty or forty-five minutes. He could do this forever and strangely, while I can't sit in a hospital room for more than a half hour without going nuts, I too could do this forever. Suddenly anything more than ten feet away from us disappears. I am entirely focused on River and the dump truck he holds in his hand, and, for the moment at least . . . I am patient.

Suggested Reading

Poetry

Wyatt, Sir Thomas. "Patience, Though I Have Not." *Sir Thomas Wyatt, the Complete Poems*, Yale University Press, 1981.

Lost in Translation

Sometimes loneliness can sneak up on you. One minute you are surrounded by friends or family, then suddenly you can feel desperately alone. Very late one night in 2013, I was sitting in the ICU waiting room while they were sorting out lines and repositioning my wife. She had just had another operation, trying to work through complications of her spinal cord tumor. The surgery had not gone well. I sat there in this large room well after midnight, no one around, with feelings of sadness and helplessness, but most of all, profound loneliness.

A nice older lady from housekeeping came in and started cleaning. She eventually worked her way near me and said hello as she worked. A minute or two later, she said something in Spanish that I did not catch, then she put her hand over her heart and looked me in the eyes. I learned that night just how isolating illness can be for patients and families, how crippling loneliness can be. I also learned how one little act of kindness can make all the difference.

Loneliness takes many forms over the different seasons of our life. It is made more painful because it often causes shame. We hide loneliness because, like the middle schooler sitting alone at a lunch table, all the world might see that we lack meaningful relationships that we assume others enjoy. We tend to hide our shame by withdrawing or isolating, often developing social anxiety or depression, leading to more withdrawal, isolation, and shame. It's a self-perpetuating cycle that can have devastating consequences.

Loneliness is usually not about being alone. Most of us have had times of loneliness, even in a crowd, even with a circle of friends and colleagues. At its core, loneliness is a lack of meaningful relationships that make us feel safe, heard, and understood. Developing these relationships becomes harder when our days are full of work and logistics, harder as we get older, harder for physicians rushing from room to room, trying to get kids to practice and homework and dinner and bed, then charting into the night. Loneliness can emerge in retirement when the daily hum of our work's activity and relationships fade, and life must be redefined.

But as I learned that night sitting alone in the ICU waiting room, loneliness associated with illness has a character all its own. Everything seems so uncertain, so out of control. Comforting routines are suddenly pulled out from under us, and the future is unknown. Ironically, as doctors, even though we understand the randomness of illness, we are often still astounded when it strikes us or a loved one, as if we should somehow be protected from it. We try to deflect our feelings by burying ourselves in the science, but in the end we are left with the stark emotional impact of it, something that those around us can help us through in a limited way. Like dying, dealing with the emotional impact of severe illness in ourselves or a close loved one is for the most part something we must do on our own. The real lesson I realized that night is how often I have been oblivious to that unique kind of pain my patients and their families experience, and how I missed opportunities to be of comfort in those tender moments ... to visibly accompany them in those hours, as I so desperately needed that night.

As I was putting together this book, I watched the movie *Lost in Translation*. It's a Bill Murray and Scarlett Johansson film about loneliness. Bill Murray plays an aging movie star spending time in Japan; he's making an obscene amount of money simply posing with a glass of whiskey. He doesn't understand the language or culture, but more importantly, he has lost touch with friends, family, and even a sense of his own identity. He tells his wife by phone that he wants to "get healthy," but doesn't seem to realize that the source of his discomfort is loneliness.

He meets another American there (Scarlett Johansson's character) with her husband who is off on photography assignments. She is also drifting, disconnected from her husband and friends. Though she finds herself shoulder to shoulder with millions of people in Tokyo, she is ironically entirely isolated. The two meet and form a community of sorts, pulling themselves at least temporarily from their loneliness and detachment. I wondered when the movie was over what became of them when they left Japan and went their separate ways. The title of the movie is a play on words and what I think it really referred to is the basic translation that we all must make between our need for connectedness and actually achieving it—the work of a lifetime.

Most of us have gone through periods of loneliness, often brought about by circumstances that punctuate any lifetime. During these periods we may or may not fully recognize what aches within us, and we would almost never admit it to someone else. Like our primordial ancestors, to not just survive but to evolve, we must somehow find our way to a seat around the warmth of the communal fire. Having found our way there, we are called on to move over and make room for someone else coming in from the cold.

Suggested Reading

Blessings

O'Donohue, John. "For Loneliness." *To Bless the Space Between Us: A Book of Blessings,* Doubleday, 2008.

Books

Whyte, David. "Alone." *Consolations: The Solace, Nourishment and Underlying Meaning of Everyday Words*, Many Rivers Press, 2021.

Poetry

Hayden, Robert. "Those Winter Sundays." *A Ballad of Remembrance*, Paul Breman, 1962.

McKay, Claude. "On Broadway." *Harlem Shadows,* Harcourt, Brace, and Company, 1922.

Kinship, Tenderness, and Being Rescued

Gregory Boyle is a Catholic priest who from scratch built what has become the largest gang rehabilitation and recovery program in the world, in the toughest neighborhoods of Los Angeles in the turbulent urban violence of the 1990s. He has written a series of three books starting with *Tattoos on the Heart* that tell the story of the program and teach us much about how people come to join gangs. More importantly, the books tell incredible, heart-wrenching, uplifting stories of how change is possible, even when it seems impossible—but only within a certain kind of community. The magic of his program is that he takes hardened gang members and finds a way to access the tender places in their hearts. These tender places exist in all of us, even those we would least expect it from. With hearts open, a sense of kinship soon develops, even among young men from rival gangs who work side by side in the programs at Homeboy Industries.

Boyle describes kinship as "not serving the other but rather being one with the other." As physicians, we all learn about this when we or a loved one become seriously ill. We quickly learn what it's like to be a patient or a family looking to our doctors for their skill, but also for hope and a sense of kinship. For most, these experiences forever after breed a kinship with our now fellow patients that changes not just the way we practice, but more importantly, how we see patients when they come to us in need of both curing and healing. Like the men and women at Homeboy Industries, when we as colleagues let our guard down and create a safe space to care for and about our colleagues, both kinship and tenderness emerge, which I have seen often in our work with physicians in distress. While it won't make our EMR (Electronic Medical Records) perform any better, or call any easier, that kinship—going arm in arm into our shared work and our lives in general, in good times and bad—can make all the difference.

For a decade after seminary, I was part of a small team that spent an evening a week with a group of men at Ministry of Challenge, a residential recovery center for unhoused men deep in the poverty of East Austin, in the days when gentrification of this area was unimaginable. Overlapping that, I met weekly with the men of Matthew House, a place of transitional housing for men just released from the maximum security prison at Huntsville. Ostensibly, these were Bible studies, but what they really were was an evening a week to explore the hidden recesses of all our lives. As different as we were in so many ways, the exploration in safe surroundings invariably revealed the kinship that Fr. Boyle describes. From this sense of kinship comes a certain kind of tenderness from people who seem to the world to be hardened, or dangerous, or hopeless—people I would never have expected it from when I started. I've learned that, just as Boyle describes, those places in the heart that allow kinship and tenderness, the ingredients of rescue, are potentially discoverable in everyone—even doctors—who in their own way sometimes find themselves on the margins of life, if it can just be uncovered and if someone cares enough to make the effort.

Living on the margins of life is different for doctors but sometimes no less distressing. The enhanced rates of suicide, depression, divorce, and addictive behavior are evidence enough of that. It's usually not economics that isolates us, but we are vulnerable to other factors. There are boundaries that by design distance us from patients in some ways, even as they are fully able and encouraged to confide in and trust us. Most of us, especially in my generation, were trained in an atmosphere that brought shame, rather than concern and mentoring, when mistakes were made, or holes in our skills or knowledge were exposed. It trained us to conceal mistakes, to hide imperfections, which is a habit that just allows it to fester. Doctors often work long hours, sometimes nights and weekends, adding another layer of isolation and resentment. Though the needle has moved some as late millennials and early Gen Z have brought a new kind of work ethic, most doctors still don't feel free to push back against poor work conditions, to express normal feelings of frustration, or get counseling when needed.

Most of you have at least some experience with volunteer work, so you know that spiritual gifts pass to all involved, not just those that the mission targets. As Boyle points out, what really defines our nourishment from this kind of work "lies not in our service to those on the margin, but in our willingness to see ourselves in kinship with them." Some of the most honest and heartfelt conversations I've ever had took place in this mission work, each with a strong sense of shared humanity. These were people who had led very different lives, most having never really been given a chance, and yet there were some universal struggles and needs that were surprisingly similar, particularly a need to feel loved and accepted regardless of our flaws. At that certain point in my life, I needed those desperate men at least as much as they needed me. A few years behind me now, I still think of some of them, even look for them at busy intersections and underpasses hoping I will not see them. They were trying to reenter an often unforgiving world, and while I told them every week just how proud of them I was, I'm not sure I ever explained to them that we were, in those hours and years, really rescuing each other.

Suggested Reading

Books

Boyle, Gregory. *Barking to the Crowd: The Power of Radical Kinship.* Simon & Schuster, 2017.

Boyle, Gregory. *Tattoos on the Heart: The Power of Boundless Compassion.* Free Press, 2010.

Poetry

Blaeser, Kimberly. "About Standing (in Kinship)." *Poetry,* Mar. 2021.

RECOVERY

Recovery

When I was in my early fifties, I finally fully realized how my father's alcohol dependence changed the course of my own life. As I went through the admissions process at the seminary where I would study for several years, the director of admissions was the first to question how my family history had affected the trajectory of my life, the road that led me to her door. I had never told her during my interviews about my father—in those days I rarely spoke of it—but she actually guessed at one point rather abruptly asking, "Which one of your parents was an alcoholic?"

I had never really read about adult children of alcoholics' somewhat predictable traits, but I had unknowingly revealed many of them as I told her about my life and faith journey. It was one of the many things I learned about myself in those years. While we are all capable of change, we are also all products of our past. Understanding our past is often essential to understanding our current lives, yet some people, like me, unknowingly avoid facing the shadows from our past.

I had a good childhood. My father was a politician and lobbyist. Even through a child's eyes, I knew he was not like the other dads, but I didn't understand that his drinking was the difference. He was not home much, but when he was there, it was mostly good things that I remember. He loved milkshakes. He taught me to play chess and gin rummy. He let me drive the golf cart when we played golf. He took me to the Astrodome when it first opened, and one night we saw Jim Wynn hit a ninth inning homer that lit up the outfield wall. The summer I was twelve, he tried to show me how to make butter like his East Texas family used to. We bought a hand-cranked churn and for a whole weekend laughed and got sore hands while we tried unsuccessfully to make butter from pasteurized milk. Three months later, he was dead.

A dozen years later, I was a medical student at Parkland in Dallas. We saw our share of patients with end-stage cirrhosis, helplessly watching the terminal phases of their awful disease, often frustrated, sometimes belittling the "choices" they had made to this end. I knew in the final week of his life my father had been transferred to Parkland where he died, and late one night I scanned rolls of ancient microfilm to find his records. What I found was that he died in much the same way as those I was caring for, and on that very same floor. I don't think anything in life has taught me more about how alike we all are—how equal—as much as we pretend differently. How fragile and flawed, and yet . . . still beautiful.

Among other things in my life, my father's story led me to our county medical society's Physician Health and Rehabilitation Committee, where I've served as chair for over a decade. I've supported scores of colleagues in recovery along with the caring specialists on our committee. It has been an interesting journey to see in an intimate way how alcohol affects so many of our colleagues and the people who love them. Most of the colleagues we support have irretrievably broken family relationships. Most are in financial ruin, many have lost their job or hospital privileges, but all who come to us for support want to protect their medical license. They want to continue to practice medicine. Alcoholism is sometimes described as a disease of broken relationships. What more perfect role can there be for a society of colleagues than to help restore a sense of right relationships with colleagues in need? It may be that our five-year sobriety success rate is high, because they desperately want to keep their license, and that's fine with me. We just want them to be whole again, to be able to start over.

Alcohol addiction is enough of a tragedy for those suffering its ravages, but by its very nature, it has profound ripple effects on virtually everyone they come in contact with. Guilt, shame, and other emotions may alter the trajectory of all involved. It is a mysterious disease. There are always unanswered questions. I seldom get to know those we follow without thinking of my father who sadly never had this kind of structured, supported recovery, and wonder what his next forty years, and mine, would have been like had he beaten his addiction. Gregory Boyle once wrote, "Just assume that the answer to every question is compassion," and so let there be compassion for those who have yet to face their addiction, for those who struggle bravely through recovery, for their colleagues and loved ones who have carried part of that burden, and when needed, for yourself.

Suggested Reading

Poetry

Oliver, Mary. "Wild Geese." *Dream Work,* Penguin, 1986.

Rumi. "The Guest House." Translated by Coleman Barks, *The Essential Rumi*, edited by Coleman Barks with John Moyne, HarperSanFrancisco, 1995.

Letting Go

People tend to get really pissed off when you confront them about their addiction. It's bad enough when it is an informal conversation of concern, predictably worse when the situation is bad enough that we must definitively intervene with an impaired colleague. I've accepted that as part of the work we do in advocating for our colleagues in recovery ... but goodness, sometimes they get really nasty. Now, I think I'm a perfectly lovely person to be around, but regardless of the collegiality, love, and concern we bring, these meetings are often contentious. The nature of addiction is to deny its existence or significance, even in the face of catastrophic consequences. In that first meeting, our colleague is often resistant, questioning our motives and denying the undeniable facts of their addiction that led to our meeting. But following our colleagues in their recovery is incredibly rewarding, leaving us with great admiration for them, particularly somewhere in those first few months when you can see that the key ingredient in recovery has taken hold: surrender. Indeed, "letting go" threads its way through the 12 Steps they will navigate. Letting go involves a difficult acknowledgement that they are not in control.

The importance of letting go is not limited to recovery. It is an ongoing process in anyone's spiritual health. The basic tenets of Buddhism—suffering, attachment, and letting go—are also expressed in other religious and spiritual disciplines. The first step, and one addicts struggle with early in recovery, is acceptance of their addiction and the power it holds over them. Most of what follows has to do with surrender of the defenses they have built to sustain their addiction. For all of us though, letting go of causes of suffering is crucial in our life journey: of attachment to things, beliefs, habits, even people. Giving up these attachments is often difficult, even painful, and is the work of a lifetime. In this sense, we share much in common with our colleagues in recovery.

I recently read Elton John's account of his own

recovery. John was fortunate to come to the point of asking for help himself. Recovery emphasizes personal responsibility but also accepting help from others. As he recalls, "We were all people who had made bad choices and had seen the consequences . . . none of us would get better without asking others for help . . . You learn to hand things over to a greater power than yourself. You have to accept that you are no longer in charge of your life."

Each of us must find our unique path to acceptance and letting go. My first experience with it was during my midlife years in seminary. The days in class were long and we would break them up with "walkabouts"—long walks around a nearby neighborhood with a classmate. On one memorable walkabout, I had an epiphany of sorts, a long overdue acceptance of childhood experiences with an alcoholic father. That day, with my friend's help, I laid that burden down, as my faith called on me to do.

There have been at least two other walkabouts that led to a similar experience. Once was on the Camino de Santiago in Spain where I randomly met a new friend, a hedge fund guy from Brazil. We developed a brother-like bond on our long walk together all the way to Finisterre where, with his help, I let go of another burden of irrational guilt and shame I had carried for years. More recently, a most unexpected friend led me on a walkabout and with their help, I again let go of another personal burden I have struggled with. Many find a path to letting go not only through other people, but through a variety of personal practices—prayer and other faith practices, meditation, journaling, exploration of nature, creative expression—the list is long.

At the heart of any kind of letting go is the desire for a better life, acceptance, surrender.

Now more than thirty years in recovery, Elton John once noted, "Sobriety is not about deprivation; it's about freedom. It's about discovering who you really are and embracing your true potential." We are all on a common journey, in turn helping those around us and needing help ourselves. I have realized, on the receiving end, that often those who have helped me the most may never know just how life changing their kindness and patience were. Colleagues and loved ones around us can confound us with their problems or behavior, addiction or otherwise, silently crying for help we can only provide if we are alert and courageous in watching out for each other. The questions posed at such times can be challenging and how we can help, or can be helped, is often unclear, but where there is love, answers appear.

Suggested Reading

Books

John, Elton. *Me.* Macmillan Publishers, 2019.

Blessings

O'Donohue, John. "For an Addict." *To Bless the Space Between Us: A Book of Blessings*, Doubleday, 2008.

In the Gloaming

Each evening after work, I walk a three mile loop from our house along the Shoal Creek trail to Pease Park and back. There's a quiet area along the trail, Custer's Meadow, separated by a few hundred yards and a steep hill from the main park. It's a meadow along the creek where General Custer and his calvary once camped, studded with ancient live oak trees, benches, and picnic tables. One evening recently, I sat down and noticed to the west a gorgeous sunset in progress, brilliant red and pink colors within the strands of clouds on a background of a deep blue sky in in the failing light.

At about the same time, along the trail came someone who looked familiar, but I couldn't quite place them. They walked over and said hello, then I remembered them from their many meetings with our county medical society's rehabilitation committee years ago as they navigated the early years of sobriety. We hugged and made small talk before they continued down the trail. For a while after they left, daylight fading to darkness, I sat in the gloaming, wondering about the larger trail that had led them to this spot. Our relationship was adversarial at first, then tempered by fire, then softened into a friendship of sorts, now cooled with time. A line from a David Whyte poem notes, "Inside everyone is a great shout of joy waiting to be born." I hope they found that voice.

It got me thinking about some of the challenges in my own life, both within and beyond my life in medicine. They have surely molded me, changed me, but most or all of that is hidden from those around me, even some of my closest friends and colleagues. Even in a life full of blessings and joy as it has been, these are problems both unique and common to us all. If we are honest, we only know a fraction of what goes on in each other's lives, and that alone should encourage grace and generosity. As a medical family, Austin is unique in how it cares for its physician community through various programs for our colleagues in recovery, in distress, and for loved ones and colleagues of those lost to suicide or other unspeakable tragedies. Much of the work is unseen, it is work that takes place on a granular level, colleague-to-colleague, as we watch out for each other, as we speak up and reach out when we sense a colleague in trouble.

In his semi-autobiographical book, *The Tennis Partner*, Abraham Verghese tells the story of a medical resident who became his close friend, then died of suicide in the grips of a cocaine addiction despite all efforts to help him. After his death someone noted, "Within your secrets lies your sickness . . . If David never sustained a lasting recovery, it was because he never let go of his secret, there were some bars that never came down. His secret is still with him. He still walks alone." Verghese notes that our peculiar profession fosters loneliness, something that greatly complicates mental health issues and recovery efforts. Verghese's sad commentary is a challenge to us to make sure that our colleagues never walk alone.

One of the basic tenets of Buddhism tells us that in the end, only three things matter: how much you loved, how gently you lived, and how gracefully you let go of things not meant for you. There are important lessons in all of these as they all apply to both our internal struggles and the way we interact with the world around us. I have far to go in all of these domains, the last one certainly the hardest. We all struggle with each of these during our lifetime, striving mightily within ourselves, all the while hoping for grace, connection, and love from those around us.

Suggested Reading

Books

Verghese, Abraham. *The Tennis Partner.* Harper Perennial, 2011.

Poetry

Whyte, David. "The Winter of Listening." *Everything is Waiting for You,* Many Rivers Press, 2003.

TRAIL MARKERS

Caduceus

One week in 2017, a colleague and I traveled to Yellow Springs, Ohio for a facilitator training workshop conducted by physician wellness pioneer Rachel Naomi Remen. We were hoping to bring her well-known "Finding Meaning in Medicine" small group program to our fledgling counseling and recovery programs. It was a transformative time spent with a collection of bright, motivated physicians mostly from prestigious institutions, who displayed exemplary vulnerability and self-examination. Their examples taught me valuable lessons. We were told prior to meeting to bring a small object from our home or office that held some symbolic significance for our work. In one of the groups, someone had brought a small caduceus lapel pin received at medical school graduation. It reminded me of the power symbols can have, emotions they can trigger, stories or habits they can remind us of.

The caduceus is the classic symbol of our profession, its usual form consisting of the familiar gold staff, wings at the top and two serpents wound around it, tangled and climbing upward. This version is different from the simpler, ancient version, the rod of Asclepius. A number of stories as to its meaning and origin exist. As Daniel Sulmasy recounts in *A Balm for Gilead: Meditations on Spirituality and the Healing Arts*, the use of caduceus is derived from a story about Asclepius, the physician hero-god of Greek mythology from whom Hippocrates claimed lineage.

According to mythology, one day Asclepius was called to help a man who had been struck by lightning. While trying to save the man's life, a snake came up beside him. Multitasking as physicians through the ages have, he quickly struck the serpent with a staff, killing it, then turned his attention back to his patient. Soon after, another snake appeared, carrying herbs in its mouth which it promptly placed in the dead snake's mouth. To the amazement of Asclepius, the dead snake was soon brought back to life. Following their example, the mythological father of medicine took some of the herbs and placed them into the mouth of his own patient who was quickly healed.

Rich in symbolism, the story makes an important point about us as physicians and as mortals. In classic literature, the snake is often a symbol of our imperfections. Within that context, we see one serpent coming to the aid of another wounded serpent, then together climbing up the staff and away from their worldly moorings, healer and healed becoming as one. We are instilled with a yearning to be like the winged staff, strong and reaching upward, but compelled to recognize that, like the serpents of this story, we are vulnerable and in need of each other. It is the humility and response to this commonality, this broken oneness with all around us, that can make us healers in the best traditions of our profession, our ethics, our faith.

On the flight home, in that rare space where we might have a couple of hours to think, I considered again the trajectory of medicine in general and my own practice in particular. We all explore, in our own way, how we might become the kind of physician, the kind of healer, that occupied our dreams as our path in medicine was being formed. The object I brought to that group that day was that list I keep of patients who have passed away over the decades. Some of the memories make me smile, for some I have regrets. When I pull the list out to make a new entry, I feel the strong desire to tell patients how I admire their courage in the face of disease, how I appreciate their trust in me and, for many, how I have cherished their friendship.

Suggested Reading

Books

Sulmasy, Daniel. *A Balm for Gilead: Meditations on Spirituality and the Healing Arts*. Georgetown University Press, 2006.

Homecomings . . . and Getting Flipped

One beautiful fall weekend in 2023, I attended the annual meeting of the Coalition for Physician Well-Being in New Mexico. As newlyweds, we lived in Albuquerque for three years during my internal medicine residency in the '80s, so it was a homecoming of sorts. Those were great years. We had our first child there and enjoyed new friends. It was beautiful, wild country ready to be explored, and New Mexico in those days was a pretty good place to be poor. It was physically and emotionally grueling, but we did it in community, in and out of the hospital, as our lives in medicine were being formed. The house we lived in is barely recognizable to me now and the two main hospitals where I worked did not resemble my days in training. In spite of the decades of change in the buildings, I found feelings of intense familiarity and connection, places that immediately evoked deep emotion and memories from those years that I look back on so fondly, days when I learned how to take care of diseases, and then how to care for people.

At the meeting, one of the talks touched briefly on EMR as a primary driver of physician distress. This speaker's topic was a more efficient way of charting office visits. The SOAP note is the classic progress note format arranged in a logical sequence: Subjective information (the patient's story of their illness), Objective observation and data, Assessment of the problem or diagnosis, and a Plan of treatment or evaluation. It works through the problem in a logical way, explaining conclusions and plans reached. This format was adopted sixty years ago; it is the gold standard for conveying medical information in an organized, predictable way and has stood the test of time. The speaker mentioned, with little fanfare or emphasis, the importance of the "flipped SOAP note."

To most of you this is old news, but to me it explained much about the often frustrating form and lack of meaningful content in some of the notes I receive from colleagues. The flipped SOAP note puts emphasis on the importance of spending most of our precious documentation time on the assessment and plan. The patient's "subjective" story of their illness is often filled in with intentional brevity, cut and pasted from the last note, or is sometimes entirely absent. When the patient's story is missing, so too is some piece of humanity from their care. Time, speed, and efficiency are paramount, the goal above and beyond all else being to reduce documentation time. The "APSO" version physically flips the order of the SOAP components, emphasizing what the reader is assumed to be primarily interested in as they hurriedly and incompletely skim the note. The implication is that the reader will seldom want to know how you reached your conclusions, only what your conclusions are. The details of the patient's personal story become secondary when time is primary.

This streamlining strategy is aimed at reducing documentation time, with the laudable goal of reclaiming time for more meaningful work or rest. There's great irony in this, as the intentional act of de-emphasizing the hearing, absorbing, and then recording the story of a person's illness—the patient's intimate, personal narrative—might actually be eliminating the key element that brings meaning to the physician-patient interaction. Two humans bond in the telling and hearing of a story, an act that moves us beyond mere data collection and into a holistic partnership. It's the process of hearing and being heard that the flipped SOAP note devalues in an era when we desperately need to find meaning in our work, where patients most of all want to be heard and have their illness put into a personal context.

Clearly, not all interactions with patients need deep connection or well-developed patient narratives, but many do, and we as doctors need it as much as our patients do. As we get more and more used to cutting documentation corners by telegraphing our patients' personal stories of illness in the race to the RVU finish line, our tendency will no doubt be to explore those things less or leave the patient story behind entirely. As David Whyte notes, "The great tragedy of speed as an answer to the complexities and responsibilities of existence is that very soon we cannot recognize anything or anyone who is not traveling at the same velocity as we are." Is this really the solution to the challenges of the EMR that we have brought upon ourselves?

The homecoming I experienced made me grateful for the countless gifts of those years, but also a little sad about what has been lost for our profession in the years since. I can now see that I am nostalgic for those days because the purity of being a doctor during training was undiluted by the practicalities of practicing medicine in the decades that would follow. Flying home across the vast West Texas desert, looking at the world and my life from 30,000 feet, I could only hope that the homecoming in my own office a few days later would carry with it some of that optimism, love, and wide-eyed curiosity that defined that time in my life. Perhaps a rediscovered gift brought home from the desert I loved in those years, now inhabited by ghosts and memories, can hopefully still inform my work today.

Suggested Reading

Articles

Whyte, David. "The Great Tragedy of Speed." *Awakin.org*.

Poetry

Sáenz, Benjamin Alire. "To the Desert." *Dark and Perfect Angels: A Collection of Poems,* Cinco Puntos Press, 1996.

Hippocrates Shrugged

In 1981, my medical school graduation took place on an outdoor plaza on campus. Hundreds of students, faculty, and family members gathered to celebrate. It was a beautiful, breezy Texas summer day, a cloudless late afternoon sky fading into evening. I vividly recall reciting the Hippocratic Oath as the sun was setting. A chill went up my spine as I realized the magnitude of our collective accomplishment. At the same time, I fully realized that I was sharing an oath taken by countless physicians through the centuries.

Hippocrates was the true pioneer of ancient medical arts and science; original fragments of the oath attributed to him date back to the third century. Both timeless and a product of his times, the earliest versions of the oath begin by swearing to a variety of Greek gods and goddesses that as a practitioner of the medical arts, certain standards would be honored.

There have been revisions through the centuries, and the modern version still used in most graduation ceremonies today dates to 1964. It is long, and if your memory is no better than mine, you probably mostly just remember that it says something about doing no harm.

As I read the modern version again after all these years, I was impressed by the fact that while the importance of scientific gains is emphasized at the very top of the oath, it primarily lists the many ways that we hold our patients' holistic wellness and dignity first and foremost. It shows how both our service to humanity, as well as the meaning and joy we find in our work, are derived from being healers. It is equally striking how the current medical environment that we work in, usually controlled by people who have never sworn this oath, makes the things that are of paramount importance in the oath almost impossible to fulfill at times. In a busy, overbooked clinic seasoned liberally with meaningless administrative tasks and onerous charting, just how easy is it to honor "... that there is art to medicine as well as science and that warmth, sympathy, and understanding may outweigh the surgeon's knife or the chemists drug"? How often do the pressures of efficiency make it difficult to "remember that I do not treat a fever chart, a cancerous growth, but a sick human being, whose illness may affect the person's family and economic stability. My responsibility includes these related problems if I am to care adequately for the sick"? Hippocrates was describing healing here, and it is embarrassing to try and explain to anyone outside of medicine about the headwinds that make honoring an oath of simply being available with humanity and healing now such a Herculean task. How can we explain it to them when we can scarcely explain to ourselves how we all too often fail to honor the essence of this oath?

There was a popular book in the '50s, *Atlas Shrugged* by Ayn Rand. The title is derived from a reference to Atlas, a Titan in Greek mythology who is remembered in myth and imagery as a giant who held the world on his shoulders. In the book, two characters have a conversation in which one asks the other what advice he would give to Atlas if the greater his effort, "the heavier the world bore down on his shoulders." The other character replied that the advice he would give would be "to shrug."

Though the title is intriguing, I never read the book and it's unclear whether to shrug means for him to express indifference or defeat to a hopeless situation, or if it means to not give up and to force his shoulders upward against the immovable force. This book title came to mind when I was considering the load that physicians carry on their shoulders these days trying to honor the Hippocratic Oath that we all swore to in a more innocent time, and how even Hippocrates himself might respond.

Our lives in medicine are often overflowing, both with things critically important and with things that are utter nonsense. It's the world we live in and the way we allow ourselves to live in it. Only when we realize this and empty our cup just enough to make room for things that are essential and true and lasting, things that we swore an oath to, that our lives in medicine might change. As Hippocrates promised, if we act to preserve the finest traditions of our calling we may "long experience the joy of healing those who seek our help."

Suggested Reading

Articles

World Medical Association. "Declaration of Geneva: Modern Version of the Hippocratic Oath." WMA, 2017.

Books

Rand, Ayn. *Atlas Shrugged.* Random House, 1957.

Remen, Rachel Naomi. *Kitchen Table Wisdom: Stories That Heal.* Riverhead Books, 1996.

Poetry

Johnson, David W. "How to be a Good Doctor on a Very Bad Day." *Physicians Anonymous,* 10 Feb. 2025.

True North

My oldest child is grown now with a career and a growing family, but he used to just be a kid, and like all children, he needed a bedtime routine. All too soon he lost interest in bedtime stories, but we still needed a way to wind down together at bedtime. In those days, a set of encyclopedias was still on the shelf, and for a while, we ended the day exploring the world together in those books. We would randomly select a volume, then flip it open to read about whatever page we landed on. It's surprising how many of those random facts I still remember today. One evening we read about "true north."

I always thought that a compass points to the North Pole. Like so many other things, I was wrong. True north is the direction along the earth's surface toward the geographic North Pole. It is almost identical to astronomical true north, calculated for centuries by ocean-bound navigators. It is a static, predictable point mariners have depended on since man began to travel.

Magnetic north is a wandering point in the Northern Hemisphere where the planet's magnetic field is vertically centered. It is the direction in which compasses point. Magnetic north varies slightly from year to year, altered by natural and man-made magnetic fields. The difference between true north and magnetic north is called declination. When we are orienting ourselves on hikes, a compass is fine, but following magnetic north as a navigation strategy over thousands of miles to precise points will inevitably cause us to become lost as ancient mariners knew. Modern navigation no longer counts on the stars; computer navigation systems orient to true north.

And so, all these years later, this fun fact I learned with my son one evening returns to haunt me (and now you) as a metaphor. In life's journey, we are often uncertain where we stand, where we are going, and what is the right path. True north is the internal compass that guides you successfully through the long road of life. It represents who you are as a human being at your deepest level. It is your point of orientation—your fixed point in a spinning world—that helps you stay on track as a leader and human being.

Your true north is based on what is most important to you: your most cherished values and beliefs, passions and motivations, the sources of satisfaction in your life. Ignoring or leaving true north unexamined is dangerous and can rob life of meaning. Being even a tiny bit off course following magnetic north, compromising any of our basic values or calling, may not seem like much in the moment, but over a lifetime, it leads us far off our intended course. Finding and following true north is the difficult work that defines our lives. When it comes to vocation, we might consider true north as another way of describing our calling—how we match what the world cries out for in need with what is deep within our heart.

I speak to physician groups frequently about burnout and wellness, and many times I have flipped through my well-worn PowerPoint slides about both. More and more it occurs to me now that most of these slides are ultimately useless unless we as individuals spend more time exploring, discovering and then tenaciously following our own unique true north.

Most of us were in small doctor-owned practices when my career began, now more than 70% of physicians are employed by larger organizations or hospitals. Often, our professional lives are influenced, if not controlled, by people far removed from the realities and sacredness of the exam room. The humanity in our work is devalued when we practice in an environment that ignores the importance of things like calling, relationships, values, respect, and meaning. Focusing most visibly on profit and market share is not putting patients first. Its wake can land us as individuals onto a rocky shoreline before we even realize we have strayed off course. Self-examination in medicine these days requires not only examining what is deep within us, but also what we allow to go on around us. If our own values and calling are in conflict with the practice or organization we work within, we go to work each day in great personal peril.

When I consider corporate medicine, megasized hospital systems, and venture capital gobbling up practices and physicians, I think the fire of calling—that was the power source for all those years of training, nights on call, days when we found ourselves truly caring for our patients—now has dwindled to just a flickering flame. But the embers are deep below, waiting to be rekindled, waiting for our profession to be saved.

Suggested Reading

Poetry

Pickthall, Marjorie. "Stars." *The Complete Poems of Marjorie Pickthal,* McClelland & Stewart, 1927.

A River Runs Through It

During that last week of 2018 when I pictured myself on a warm beach or by a fire in the mountains, I instead found myself, along with my loyal but somewhat annoyed staff, manually entering "Quality" and "Improvement Activities" data to satisfy my MIPS (Merit-Based Incentive Payment System) requirement to avoid Medicare penalties two years down the road. Many of you will have no idea what I am talking about, as your practice managers and EMR silently take care of this each year. But for those increasingly rare souls in small practices wary from hearing complaints about "pajama time" and the other struggles and cost of maintaining an EMR, that tedious time at the end of the year somehow seemed worth it. I wondered if clinging to my paper charts was a reasonable strategy or if I'm just the proverbial old man hollering at kids to get off my lawn. So much misery in medicine has been caused by EMRs that I'm convinced that in solo practice where there is much to lose and little to gain, avoiding an EMR was soul saving.

At conception, MACRA's QPP (Quality Payment Program) was supposedly part of the pathway to value-based medicine. There is, of course, nothing wrong with the idea that being paid to keep people healthy is a better idea for society than primarily paying us to do things for people after they are sick. What I couldn't get out of my mind was the repeated reference to *value*. Not surprisingly, the word *values* is never mentioned. In fact, many argue that the very source of what is wrong with medicine, and more specifically with doctors, has everything to do with *values*, and not nearly as much to do with *value*.

There are certain values that can be traced back to the origins of medicine—ideas like fidelity, compassion, competence, kindness, respect, and calling to name a few—that make us the healing profession that we are. Many say that physician distress and burnout are the direct results of working in a system that provides little or no incentive, often even obstacles, to honoring core values of our profession. This time of year, when I am most acutely aware of distractions that distance us from honoring values sacred to our profession, I am reminded of a quote from Goethe: "Things which matter most must never be at the mercy of things that matter least."

There is a river that connects physicians of antiquity to us in our own time, and beyond. The shores that the river endlessly passes are the ever-changing shores of advancing science and evolving economics. Both surely change the façade of medicine in every age and will continue to do so in ways we can scarcely imagine today. But the river itself carries with it certain timeless truths, values that are the same in any age, even if often hidden beneath rushing currents. The river burnishes and refines the stones in its bed, stones that carry messages that if not sought out and given homage, remain hidden at our own peril. These are words of timeless wisdom from our predecessors that we must both receive and pass on. My favorite line from a lifetime of reading is from Norman Maclean's *A River Runs Through It*. It reminds me of being mindful of the heritage passed on through the lineage of medicine: "Eventually all things merge into one, and a river runs through it. The river was cut by the world's great flood and runs over rocks from the basement of time. On some of the rocks are timeless raindrops. Under the rocks are the words and some of the words are theirs."

In seminary, we often spoke of the "cloud of witnesses," wise and faithful people who both created and preserved our rich traditions of faith through the centuries. I often think of our predecessors in medicine who have done the same for us as physicians. They are our guides on this long road, and we ignore their wisdom at great peril to ourselves, our patients, and our profession. Their words, and ours, pass from generation to generation, preserve our best traditions, timelessly echo our quest for healing, and call on us to honor our rich lineage.

Suggested Reading

Books

Goethe, Johann Wolfgang von. *Maxims and Reflections.* Macmillan, 1833.

Maclean, Norman. "A River Runs Through It." *A River Runs Through It and Other Stories,* University of Chicago Press, 1976.

Unleashed

I read an essay by poet Mary Oliver recently that describes her childhood home. Dogs roamed free until town ordinances required leashing, and a dog catcher was hired. One particular dog, Sammy, was sort of a communal pet and did not take well to leashing. He would show up repeatedly in her yard, a chewed-through leash dragging behind him, unwilling to be tied. She eventually adopted him. After appearing before a judge for being unable to keep the dog confined, she built a fence, which he promptly learned to climb. It's a story about natural instincts to refuse unnatural constraints.

It made me think of medicine through the ages, but more specifically the last few decades. Now our profession faces immense challenges to remain a healing profession, rather than just being swallowed up by economic forces that have positioned the bottom line first. Patient and physical well-being is almost an afterthought. As a profession and as healers, we have been leashed in many ways over the years, even as medical science and all of its miracles have emerged. Particularly in the years during and following the pandemic, we learned to recognize and respect that each of us has a certain uneasiness that we often can't quite put into words. As skilled observers of the human condition, we have come to recognize its effects on our patients and our colleagues, perhaps better than we recognize it in ourselves. At the height of the pandemic, author David Kessler noted, "That discomfort you're feeling is grief." Grief for things lost that we had not even realized were important to us.

While young physicians entering practice in those years have never known any better, most of us feel the effects of the incremental but seismic changes in how we are forced to "deliver care" these days. However we describe it, like other constraints imposed by the systems we work within, some aspects threaten to pull us away from what ultimately energizes us as physicians—a sense of meaning. But as a good friend pointed out as I was writing this, too often we overlook the good things that we realized in the pandemic: the gifts, the resetting of our personal outlook and tolerances. Perhaps it's also a good time to acknowledge that some of the leashes we struggle against are self-imposed, bonds to be broken only through self-examination and, yes, resilience.

A study from several years ago set out to answer the question, "What do doctors find meaningful about their work?" Studying narratives written by volunteers, they found three recurring themes: a fundamental change in perspective, connection with patients, and making a difference in someone's life. Change of perspective typically occurred after being part of a profound emotional experience shared with a patient. Connection with patients was described as occurring over hours or decades, involving moments of emotional intimacy and the doctor's willingness to respond personally and genuinely. Making a difference in someone's life was not usually from brilliant diagnostic insight or skilled therapeutic intervention. Rather it involved stories occurring in the setting of chronic, incurable illness, situations in which a doctor's healing presence was itself therapeutic and showed true empathy.

Common to each is recognition that sickness includes both disease, a disturbance of the body that needs our technical skills, and also illness, a disturbance of the soul that requires healing—humanity and connection—and therein lies the real meaning in our work. Each of these themes requires the physician to be undistracted and present in the moment, something difficult in most day-to-day practice settings. When we think about meaning in those terms, it is easy to see how so many things that distract us from meaningful work may obscure recognition of moments that should energize us, make us better doctors, better human beings.

As for Mary Oliver's Sammy, eventually, as he aged, he was harmless, but no more likely to allow himself to be confined, and the town turned a blind eye to his wanderings. The dog catcher who had rounded him up so many times quit; his career was outlived by Sammy's persistence. Unencumbered, she notes, "In this way, he lived a long and happy life." Physicians through the ages, never more so than today, have looked for ways to break free of the leashes that distract, even separate us from finding meaning in our work, too often unsuccessfully. But meaning is still there, at times hidden, waiting to be rediscovered. The pandemic subsided and in the short term at least, there was gratitude, new priorities and perspectives, appreciation for the return of things so easily lost, lessons learned, unexpected gifts received, and from that at least we were unleashed. It was, of course, replaced increasingly by other constraints, but in that moment, we recognized what Mary Oliver describes as "the wonderful things that may happen if you break the ropes that are holding you." Perhaps from that, there is hope for the future.

Suggested Reading

Articles

Berinato, Scott. "That Discomfort You're Feeling is Grief." *Harvard Business Review,* 23 Mar. 2020.

Horowitz, Carol, et al. "What Do Doctors Find Meaningful About Their Work?" *Annals of Internal Medicine,* vol. 138, no. 9, 2003, https://pmc.ncbi.nlm.nih.gov/articles/PMC4303370/.

Books

Oliver, Mary. *Upstream: Selected Essays.* Penguin, 2016.

Medicine as a Spiritual Practice

Rachel Naomi Remen, pioneer in the physician wellness movement, once spoke about her grandfather, whom she describes as a Jewish mystic and an enduring influence in her life. In an emotional interview, she fondly recalls that when she was a child he told her a story of the creation of the world and the great lesson from it. It was the story of the "birthday of the world," its beginning emerging as a sacred act of creation from darkness. She wrote, "And then in the course of history, at a moment in time, this world, the world of a thousand thousand things, emerged from the heart of the holy darkness as a great ray of light ... and the vessel containing the light of the world—the wholeness of the world—broke and the wholeness of the world, the light of the world, was scattered into a thousand thousand fragments of light and ... We are here because we are born with the capacity to find the hidden light in all events and all people, to lift it up and make it visible once again ..."

As physicians, we are in a unique position to be part of this calling, to heal one heart at a time. To do so in our professional lives, we must practice at the intersection of science and spirituality, more often described as the intersection between curing and healing. We have the privilege and responsibility of being witness to our patients' physical and spiritual challenges laid bare before us, and some would argue that one of our most frequent failings is to focus wholly on science, paying little attention to the spiritual needs of our patients.

Spirituality might be looked at as beliefs and practices, even stories, that respond to a shared human need for meaning. It is a model, a framework, for life based on belief that beyond what our senses reveal to us, there is a greater transcendent presence yet to be fully discovered. It is admittedly delicate landscape to explore with patients, especially as we first come to know them.

There are thousands of Medline articles about spirituality and medicine. Numerous studies demonstrate patients' longing for physicians to inquire about their spiritual beliefs and needs, just as surely as studies demonstrate how seldom we respond to this. We know that a patient's engagement with their own unique spirituality has demonstrable benefits to health and wholeness that complement the science we bring to the bedside. And yet, far too often we simply ignore its power, leaving it tragically unattended. Surveys have revealed many reasons for this, not the least of which is the time it takes in the middle of a busy clinic. How have we descended into a system that allows barely enough time to get the science part done, the curing, making it nearly impossible to adequately address the spiritual, the healing?

Later in the same interview, Remen recalls the early days of her career. Plagued with chronic health problems herself, she developed a kind of compassion, a keen awareness of the spiritual needs of her patients that launched a career providing a unique kind of care for cancer patients. She said, "I began to realize how I had been healed by these people with cancer, how I had moved from a person focused on curing and coming to understand that we are all healers of one another. That people have been healing each other since the beginning, and that my power to cure was only a small part of my power to help people." To heal and to be healed in our work—it is perhaps the most crucial cycle in the practice of medicine that keeps us as physicians engaged, empathetic, and spilling over with love of our work and our patients.

Suggested Reading

Books

Remen, Rachel Naomi. *The Birthday of the World: A Story About Finding Light in Everyone and Everything.* Abrams Books for Young Readers, 2022.

Podcast Transcripts

Trippett, Krista, host. "Dr. Rachel Naomi Remen: The Difference Between Curing and Healing." *On Being,* 8 Apr. 2020.

Videos

Sulmasy, Daniel. "Is Health Care a Spiritual Discipline?" HDS HMS Lecture Series on Religion and Medicine, 25 Sep. 2013, Harvard Divinity School. Lecture.

Standing on
Holy Ground

One of my favorite passages from sacred writings is the story of Moses, still tending his father-in-law's sheep on an ordinary day in an ordinary place. He suddenly encounters God, and the ground he stood on is now consecrated into holy ground. He is admonished, "Take off your sandals, for the place you are standing is holy ground." All the world's religions speak of holy ground. For Muslims, even the simplest prayer rug in the humblest of places becomes holy ground to commune with Allah. Buddhists may have a transcendent experience at a stupa. The concept of holy or sacred ground transcends religion and in a secular sense, people commonly find themselves encountering a different spiritual plane in all kinds of places. The experience may sneak up on you, and it requires open eyes to be receptive to it.

Some years back, my wife had an appointment with a specialist at Southwestern Medical School in Dallas where we would receive more news about a diagnosis that would forever change our lives in so many ways. While she was waiting to be seen, I went back to the medical school auditorium where I spent so many transformative hours all those years ago. The room had many technological upgrades over the years, but it was still much the same. I considered my own time there and the fact that the doctors Maryann saw next door all would have either trained or taught in this same room. I had a sense of an almost mystical nature of this ordinary room, of all the lives changed for those who passed through its doors. Similarly, a patient of mine just a few days earlier had described such a feeling when visiting the military cemetery at Normandy. These spaces can outwardly be ornate or very ordinary, but they are ground that becomes extraordinary and carries with it a moment in which we seem to commune with something beyond ourselves: visiting a favorite place in nature, working in a food bank, quietly nursing a baby.

So how might we describe holy ground in ways that may be recognizable, even familiar to all of us, regardless of whether we appreciate its presence with religious, spiritual, or purely secular eyes? Some describe it as a "thin place," a place the Celtic tradition describes as a place where the space between the material and the divine becomes very small. There the concrete merges with the infinite. There our tangible, practical world is suddenly enveloped with mystery and transcendent truth. Where, for a time, we feel untethered and are united with a hidden world and souls around us. As with Moses, the terrain itself may be ordinary, but what happens upon it, or what it comes to signify makes it sacred.

In healthcare, presumably there was an original sense of calling to heal, a calling that you answered years ago and still follow. For all of the things that get in the way of us pursuing it well, we are still incredibly privileged to inhabit the holy ground on which we meet our patients, people on a common journey with us, who literally and figuratively bare their bodies and souls before us, with trust—with an assumption that we will come to them with humanity, compassion, and fidelity—to stand on this ground. As we do, we agree to leave behind the encumbrances and baggage that we all carry. For the moment, we leave it all at the entrance to this sacred and mysterious space.

Pause at the door, take a cleansing breath, then enter the exam room, ER cubicle, or operating room. Take off your sandals; you are standing on holy ground.

Suggested Reading

Poetry

Whyte, David. "The Opening of Eyes." *Songs For Coming Home,* New Rivers Press, 1989.

Scripture

The Bible, *Exodus 3:1-5*

FIRM FOOTING

Writing a Wrong

Twenty-five years ago, just a couple of years before tort reform became a reality in Texas, I faced the only malpractice suit of my career. It was in the days when few doctors were untouched by malpractice litigation. On the day that an armed constable arrived unannounced in my office with court documents, I was devastated, humiliated, and shocked. I was an innocent bystander in the suit; about a year into it, the judge unceremoniously dropped me from the case, but not until I had gone through a year of worry, anguish, sleepless nights, and self-doubt. The patient, who died of widely metastatic colon cancer, was a kind, soft-spoken man with severe rheumatoid disease. He was usually accompanied by his wife and daughter, and I grew close to them in the years that I cared for him, making being named in the suit even more painful.

Forbidden by attorneys to discuss the case with colleagues, I nonetheless did speak with a close friend and mentor who urged me to give voice to this hidden pain, either with counseling or journaling. I was entirely unfamiliar with journaling, including expressive writing (reflective writing that explores thoughts and feelings surrounding traumatic or stressful experiences), but after some cursory research, I gave it a try. For me, expressive writing has been a life-changing exercise that I continue to this day

There are countless articles and books that support a myriad of physical and mental health benefits of journaling. Dr. James Pennebaker, professor emeritus and psychology researcher at UT Austin, was an early pioneer in this research. He began his research decades ago when he tested out the benefits of expressive writing with college students. His early studies demonstrated a clear correlation between past traumatic experiences and current physical health measures, including frequency of infections and hospitalizations, persisting for years after the trauma. He developed studies in which he asked student participants to write about a traumatic experience in their life for just fifteen minutes a day on four consecutive days. Those who participated subsequently visited student health services only half as frequently as the control group. This led to a flood of studies in subsequent years showing the benefits of expressive writing in all kinds of mental and physical health domains.

Over the decades that have followed, Dr. Pennebaker has offered concrete advice for people wishing to pursue this beneficial practice. He advises that expressive writing should deal with our most traumatic or stressful experiences (current or past), as well as things that you might be worrying about too much or issues adversely affecting your life or relationships. He recommends that over a few days you write about this experience, bringing to light your deepest emotions and thoughts related to it. Fifteen minutes a day is plenty. Even as little as two minutes can be effective, as there is residual processing after the pen is set down. He emphasizes that writing should be for your eyes only to promote honesty and deep reflection.

When you have completed writing, you may want to save it, but it's fine, even encouraged, to literally and symbolically destroy it. He recommends doing this as needed, rather than a daily practice, to help you deal with experiences that you sense are being allowed to fester. It's free, not particularly time consuming, and for most who practice, it can be liberating, even life changing.

It's on my mind this month as I came across the box of records, court notices, and personal notes about the case from all those years ago. It all finally went into our shred box, bound for HIPAA heaven. Strangely enough, even as I set it all aside for good, I couldn't help feeling a certain fondness for this quiet, humble man who I came to know well in those years. In this big, beautiful life that we have been given, there are inevitably profound traumatic events, seemingly insurmountable challenges, mistakes, and regret. There are many effective ways of dealing with these challenges: deep connection with others, counseling, meditation, prayer/faith, journaling. Within each of us, there are deeply held experiences that we avoid confronting, that hold us back. That's just part of the human condition. Among the many gifts that we have been given is the ability, if we are willing, to turn and face the shadows that haunt us, then to discern our own unique and sustainable path forward to wholeness.

Suggested Reading

Books

Kabat-Zinn, Jon. *Full Catastrophe Living: Using the Wisdom of Your Body and Mind to Face Stress, Pain, and Illness.* Random House, 1990.

Podcasts

Mills, Kim, host. Expressive writing can help your mental health, with James Pennebaker, PhD. *Speaking of Psychology,* episode 277, American Psychological Association, Mar. 2024, https://www.apa.org/news/podcasts/speaking-of-psychology/expressive-writing.

Poetry

Oliver, Mary. "I Worried." *Swan,* Beacon Press, 2012.

Three Trout and Wisdom From the Ordinary

Let's be honest about something that people are notoriously dishonest about: fishing. I am just a terrible fisherman. I'm no good at picking bait. I'm impatient. I try to set the hook too early or too late. I can't read the water in a Colorado stream, nor see redfish swirling in the bay at the coast. Some years back, I decided to take up fly fishing after re-reading Norman Maclean's *A River Runs Through It*, thinking I might fare better. We vacationed in Lake City, Colorado back then, and I managed to catch two nice trout one memorable afternoon. However, I'd have to say the day ended in a draw because I also hooked my fishing hat twice. I feel pretty sure that my father-in-law, a great outdoorsman, went to his grave wondering why in the world his daughter married such a terrible fisherman.

With our adult children and six grandchildren recently in Port Aransas, I was determined to catch some fish with my eight-year-old grandson. There was a lake behind the house and we fished it some that first day, but all we managed to catch was a very unfortunate turtle. I gave in and hired a guide for some bay fishing, but when we got to the dock that morning, there was a message that he had called in sick. You don't tell an eight-year-old that a fishing trip is called off, so on advice from a local in the bait shop, we went to a spot where we could fish from a pier or wade.

What followed was at once predictable and surprising. My grandson caught a croaker, just a bit bigger than what we could buy at the bait store. As I was about to throw it back, he wanted to look at it. He marveled at the different colors that glistened in the sunlight, the spines, the pumping gills. Over the next hour or so, we caught three small trout, none of them keepers, but he was amazed at how slippery they were and laughed as they repeatedly squirmed from his grasp when he tried to throw them back.

By mid-morning, nothing was biting, but several dolphins joined us just a few feet away much to his amazement. In the end, a fishing trip that I would have called a dismal failure was a great time that he talked about for days. It was only one of many times that week when ordinary things—collecting shells, letting his feet sink into sand in the surf, feeding seagulls—things I hardly notice anymore, fascinated him, and through him, became visible again to me.

The evening before we left, I snuck out to the lake at dusk to try my luck again. It was a still evening, a full moon rising, and the little lake was smooth as glass. John Buchan famously wrote, "The charm of fishing is that it is the pursuit of what is elusive but attainable, a perpetual series of occasions for hope," a quote that fits even unsuccessful fishing well, and life in general. The casts were well placed, or so I thought, the results predictable but soothing nonetheless. I stood there in the quiet of early evening, Norman Maclean style, in the half-light where, however briefly, "all existence fades to being with my soul . . . and the hope that a fish will rise." Perhaps there is more fisherman in me than I thought, seeing the essence of fishing before me,

Three Trout and Wisdom from the Ordinary • 195

even without fish. I stood there and considered the lessons of that week—that there is wisdom in the ordinary, and with each cast, hope.

Suggested Reading

Books

Buchan, John. *Great Hours in Sport.* Thomas Nelson & Sons, 1921.

Chittister, Joan. *Wisdom Distilled from the Daily: Living the Rule of St. Benedict Today.* HarperOne, 2009.

Poetry

Dickinson, Emily. "Hope is the thing with feathers." *The Poems of Emily Dickinson*, edited by R. W. Franklin, Belknap Press, 2005.

The Imposter

My first job in Austin, way back in the 1980s, was with a multispecialty clinic where many of the best internal medicine specialists practiced. It was an intimidating place for a rookie, and I was nervous and self-conscious those first few months. Late one Friday afternoon, I got a call from one of our internists on their way out the door, asking me to see one of their patients before I signed out. It was a difficult problem, the referring doctor was unreachable, and in the end, I had to find a surgeon to assess the patient in the ER. This was an era when a good doctor didn't just send a patient to the ER without arranging care at the other end. The next week, we were gathered at the hospital for a quarterly staff meeting, and in front of a dozen of my new colleagues, the referring partner berated me for referring their patient to a surgeon they didn't usually work with. I tried to explain, but they cut me off and repeated their angry and dismissive warning. I had been scolded like a child, and there was an awkward silence as I was revealed to be a fraud, an imposter, who didn't know how things were supposed to be done. It sounds silly, even trivial now, but at the time it was devastating.

Imposter syndrome was originally described in the 1970s by Pauline Clance and Suzanne Imes as an "internal experience of intellectual phoniness . . . It is usually witnessed in individuals who seem successful to others, but on the inside, they feel incompetent." A 2022 study from Stanford surveyed 3,000 physicians and found that 1 in 4 experienced frequent or intense impostor syndrome symptoms. The study author, Tait Shanafelt, notes that U.S. physicians are at an 80% increased risk for the syndrome relative to people with a doctoral or professional degree in another field. He notes that in its worst forms, impostor syndrome carries a greater risk of occupational burnout, profound work dissatisfaction, depression, even suicidal thoughts, resulting in loss of effectiveness and loss of meaning in their work.

While it is prevalent across the demographic

spectrum, imposter syndrome was originally described as a syndrome primarily affecting women, and though it can profoundly affect either sex, it may do so in different ways. Dr. Valerie Young, author of *The Secret Lives of Successful Women And Men: Why Capable People Suffer from Impostor Syndrome and How to Thrive In Spite of It*, notes that gender differences that are present in this syndrome are often created by persistent differences in the way society judges men and women. She notes that society has often "forced fit" men into a certain definition of success generally measured in terms of money, power, and status. However, measuring success is often more complex in professional women, especially those with children, where there are several success domains at play simultaneously. She describes that women often "have a more layered definition of success . . . that also includes meaning, balance, and relationships."

There are many strategies for managing imposter syndrome. Dr. Young notes that at the core of them is humility—making peace with imperfections and limitations while recognizing and reinforcing the intelligence, talent, and love that we work so hard bring to work with us.

She writes, "I think that's one of the most important parts of recovering from this... saying 'I don't know' and being OK with uncertainty, which is especially difficult in medicine." One simple exercise is to put a Post-It note in a prominent spot at our desk that reminds us of the strength, sacrifice, accomplishments, and caring we bring to our patients, even with imperfections. Being honest about self-doubt with close colleagues can be helpful. For some, counseling can be a lifeline that provides much needed insight, perspective, and effective strategies.

I composed this sitting in a church waiting for a funeral to start. This is the third funeral I've attended this year, two earlier ones being close friends who lost long, difficult battles with cancer. For each, there were a couple of weeks at the end in hospice care—in transition—lucidity fading, briefly inhabiting what Celtic tradition calls a "thin place," a liminal space where Heaven and Earth very nearly merge into one. Ironically, even as I considered the concept of death, I was also able to give a prayer of thanks, for in just a few weeks our eighth grandchild would be born. Birth and death—the very bookends of our lives in this world. At each of these extremes, life is distilled to its simplest, most essential elements, our souls laid bare: pure, loved, forgiven. How do all those years in between become so complicated, our expectations of ourselves so distorted, that feeling like an imposter is even possible?

Suggested Reading

Articles

Clance, Pauline, and Suzanne Imes. "Imposter Phenomenon in High Achieving Women: Dynamics and Therapeutic Intervention." *Psychotherapy: Theory, Research, and Practice,* vol. 15, no. 3, 1978, pp. 241-247.

Shanafelt, Tait, et al. "Imposter Phenomenon in US Physicians Relative to the US Working Population." *Mayo Clinic Proceedings,* vol. 97, no. 11, 2022, pp. 1981-1993.

Books

Brown, Brené. *The Gifts of Imperfection: Let Go of Who You Think You're Supposed to Be and Embrace Who You Are.* Hazelden, 2010.

Young, Valerie. *The Secret Thoughts of Successful Women: And Men: Why Capable People Suffer from Impostor Syndrome and How to Thrive In Spite of It.* Crown Currency, 2011.

Poetry

Rumi. "Come Back My Soul." Translated by Coleman Barks, *The Essential Rumi*, edited by Coleman Barks with John Moyne, HarperSanFrancisco, 1995.

Mending Wall

At a volunteer clinic years ago, past our usual quitting time, they kept letting patients check in. It's an evening clinic and after a long day, I was getting grumpy about staying late. A colleague and fellow Methodist set me straight (or was he just messing with me?) by reminding me of a quote often attributed to John Wesley. "Do all the good you can, by all the means you can, in all the ways you can, in all the places you can, at all the times you can, for all the people you can, as long as ever you can," Wesley said. Thanks to that night, I often remember this call to infinite service and not with fondness. While it's low-hanging fruit for a sermon, it would likely elicit groans in a doctor's dining room. Physician wellness today focuses on recognizing healthy boundaries.

It was on my mind again as I read Melissa Urban's book, *The Book of Boundaries: Set the Limits*

That Will Set You Free. Urban's theme is that setting boundaries in all phases of our lives leads to peace and happiness in relationships, work, and with ourselves. Many of us go through life unhappy in one or all of these domains because we fail to declare boundaries, instead assuming those around us will read our minds, then honor these invisible lines. She notes three stages of setting boundaries: first, discerning what boundaries are important to us, then clearly, kindly, and verbally informing those affected, and last, by enforcing them. She emphasizes that setting boundaries is an act of love; it ultimately strengthens relationships and makes us more effective in the workplace. Defining boundaries should come from a place of love. The point of them should never be to control or change those around us, rather to define behaviors and actions we will or won't tolerate in our own lives.

Some boundaries for doctors are obvious, such as unprofessional relationships with a patient or employee—anyone with whom we have an unequal power dynamic—or treating those with whom we have a relationship that might cloud our medical judgement. But Urban goes far beyond these obvious examples. At work, many, if not most, of our colleagues are asked to see too many patients, do too much work at home, and have too little control over their schedules, often at great cost to loved ones and themselves. Ironically, while we are confident and clear with our patients, we may feel strangely powerless to set boundaries for how we navigate our workday, or fail to enforce boundaries we do set, then wonder why we are miserable at work.

Setting boundaries with friends and family can take many forms—anything that puts us repeatedly in situations we find awkward or against our values. Toxic relationships with family or friends ("vampire friends") are just not worth the effort if they perpetually ignore boundaries. We hear all too often from married people, especially those with young children, the laments of unequal parenting duties, unequal "me" time, too little "we" time, complaints of dissatisfaction with all kinds of issues related to physical and emotional intimacy. Our experience in our counseling program speaks strongly to the fact that physicians seek help related to relationships as much or more than issues solely related to their work; many of those work issues are clearly linked to our failure to establish and follow boundaries healthy for us.

Perhaps most important are the boundaries that we should set for ourselves. It can be simple things related to diet, exercise, time spent at work, or time we gift ourselves and loved ones. These are boundaries we need to keep mentally and physically healthy. The inability to say "no" is a common personal boundary we often neglect. When we fall into the trap of taking on too much from all that people ask of us, it is not their fault. It is our fault for not setting personal boundaries and then following them. As Urban points out, if you never say no, ". . . they are never going to stop asking. Why should they?"

Robert Frost's 1914 poem, "Mending Wall," contains one of the most frequently quoted lines in American poetry: "Good fences make good neighbors." The poem's interpretations are nuanced and evolved in the era of world wars that followed its writing, but the line itself is timeless. Perhaps boundaries, like good fences, when brought with love help us live in harmony and peace. Boundary setting is a sign of maturity and respect for the important relationships with ourselves and others. As Urban notes, "... Boundaries produce the shiniest version of ourselves. They say, 'I am worth protecting.'"

Suggested Reading

Books

Urban, Melissa. *The Book of Boundaries: Set the Limits That Will Set You Free*. The Dial Press, 2022.

Poetry

Frost, Robert. "A Time to Talk." *Mountain Interval*, Henry Holt and Company, 1916.

Frost, Robert. "Mending Wall." *North of Boston*, David Nutt, 1914.

Goliath

Since childhood, one of my favorite stories is David and Goliath—the story of the young future king who finds himself by a combination of chance and choice facing the Philistine giant. The fate of David's army depends on him alone, with only his wits, faith, and courage to perform a seemingly impossible feat. We might all identify with this story, as we have felt ourselves to be an underdog at some point in our lives.

As someone who has spent a long career in solo or two doctor practices, I've felt a little like David more than once, especially recently in controversy with a big insurance carrier posing a significant threat to my small practice. Insurers are indeed the modern day Goliaths in healthcare. While large hospital systems and venture capital funded mega-practices must fight battles of scale, they have resources to mount a decent defense. Small mom and pop practices like mine fight with limited resources against great odds. Many would suggest that perhaps all of this is a sign that my small practice model is simply experiencing the Darwinian extinction it deserves, but I am not willing to give up on it and the closeness it brings for me with my patients. As it happens, I was preparing a Sunday School lesson about David and Goliath not long ago and came across an essay about the "monomyth" or "the Hero's Journey." Described by author Joseph Campbell and others, the Hero's Journey is a basic story pattern throughout mythology, a pattern frequently found in other ancient writings as well as later day literature and film.

The structure of the Hero's Journey is as follows: the hero from the ordinary world is called to adventure. After initially refusing the call, they cross the threshold into a supernatural region. They descend into "the belly of the whale" and "the road of trials," along the way meeting with helpers, mentors, deities, temptations, and seemingly insurmountable challenges. There is atonement with a higher power, then receipt of the treasure and apotheosis (achievement of a higher level of existence), finally rebirth and return to the ordinary world, now possessing gifts to bestow on humanity.

Literature is often a reflection of everyday life, and if we spend a little time thinking about it, we may be able to see many small, and perhaps a few large, monomyths in our own lives. We sometimes lose track of just how hard it is to practice medicine. We pass through a certain threshold from our early lives into a life of medicine, lives that are full of mentors, challenges, temptations, and perhaps dark times spent traveling the "road of trials." But like the heroes in many of the stories, as we navigate difficult times in our careers, and our lives in general, the treasure that we acquire may be peace and a certain kind of knowledge. Perhaps even wisdom—treasure we desperately need to receive from others to guide us through life, and, in kinship, we are in turn called on to share with colleagues, loved ones, and patients. It is indeed heroic to achieve and then share the gifts that we attain on these journeys, which are anything but ordinary, but sometimes come at great cost. Receiving these precious gifts from wise friends and mentors has made all the difference in my life.

Different authors describe the Hero's Journey

in different ways, but all include the importance of the "mentor" or "supernatural aid" that assists in the journey. We may find this assistance in several ways. One is deep within our own souls, beyond ego where our deepest desires and meaning live, a place it takes some effort to reach. Another is found within our community of colleagues, bound together with common hopes and goals, supporting each other, sometimes going arm in arm down the road of trials, then hopefully beyond. For many of us, it is a sense of a transcendent presence. All of these may be woven together on life's defining journeys. With the help of a most unlikely friend, I've put my practice crisis into perspective, at least for the moment. I have been blessed in this life, and each day offers too much to waste it in worry. Easy to say, harder to live. Perhaps the real Goliath here is not the insurance company, rather it's my reaction to it, letting it be a giant inhabiting my soul, lurking in the shadows. I'm no hero, but that's a Goliath I might just beat.

On my desk, there's a fortune from a fortune cookie with a well-known saying: "Act boldly and unseen forces will come to your aid." It is a call to a dynamic life of action and mission but also recognizes that we all need help. We are called to be forward looking, even as we carry lessons of the past with us on the journey in order to act boldly and offer our gifts and dreams to a world in need. Like the Hero's Journey, your life lived boldly will include treasure and homecomings, but also trials and tragedy ... but what epic story, what grand tapestry of life, doesn't?

Suggested Reading

Books

Gladwell, Malcolm. *David and Goliath: Underdogs, Misfits, and the Art of Battling Giants.* Little, Brown and Company, 2013.

Poetry

Angelou, Maya. "Still I Rise." *And Still I Rise*, Random House, 1978.

The Cosmic Dance

Joseph Campbell was a writer best known for *The Hero with a Thousand Faces*, which describes the literary theory of the hero's journey, shared by world mythologies and often found in contemporary works of literature and film. He famously conducted a workshop in which physicians were shown the classic "Dancing Shiva" statue. In the statue, Shiva, the Hindu God, is dancing in a ring of flames. The hands of his many arms are shown holding symbols signifying the abundance of spiritual life. As he dances, one leg is lifted high and the other is standing on the back of a man crouched in the dirt, typically depicted as staring at a leaf that he holds in his hand. Rachel Naomi Remen quotes Campbell as asking his audience, "What is that little guy down there doing?" After giving physicians in the room time to ponder the question, he answered it himself: "That's a little man who is so caught up in the study of the material world that he does not notice that the living God is dancing on his back."

I especially appreciate this story when I'm around our grandchildren, whose unfiltered honesty and innocent perspective sometimes stops me in my tracks with sheer insight coming from the mouth of a child. One Thanksgiving I experienced such a memorable example. It is, of course, a tradition that calls on us to look up from our daily routines and give thanks, which requires that we have an awareness—a presence—to recognize just how miraculous our blessings really are. Like many of you, we gather at our Thanksgiving table, and before we offer our prayer of thanks, we go around and ask each person, old and young, to tell us what they are thankful for. The responses are usually somewhat predictable, even if heartfelt. Once when our children were very young, one of our daughters, with everyone staring at her in anticipation, nervously paused then blurted out that she was thankful for "life!" It has stuck with me these last few months as simultaneously being a simple, yet all-encompassing expression of thanksgiving, given through the lips of a child. Embracing gratitude as a daily practice, rather than just one day a year, nourishes us, makes us measurably happier, and puts life's inevitable disappointments into perspective.

In its purest form, gratitude helps us, at least for the moment, to set aside the things that make us anxious or sad or wanting, and looks at the essence of joy, of what makes our lives rich and worthy of living. It reboots our fearfully overloaded hard drives and propels us into the world of chaos with a smile and courage, knowing full well that it is a process that we must repeat frequently to remain sane, perhaps even joyful.

Thomas Merton, a Trappist monk, theologian, poet, and mystic wrote extensively about gratitude to a worldwide following. Merton noted that gratitude helps us to shed what he called the "awful solemnity" of life and to dance into something that our lives are intended to be: "The more we persist in misunderstanding the phenomena of life ... the more we involve ourselves in sadness, absurdity and despair. But it does not matter much, because no despair of ours can alter the reality of things, or stain the joy of the cosmic dance which is always there ...

the fact remains that we are invited to forget ourselves on purpose, cast our awful solemnity to the winds, and join in the general dance."

Said differently in a child's blessing one Thanksgiving, gratitude makes our hearts dance daily in joyful celebration of the very gift of life.

Suggested Reading

Articles

Venkataraman, Swami. "The symbolism of Nataraja, the Cosmic Dancer." *Hindu American Foundation,* 16 Feb. 2022.

Books

Merton, Thomas. *New Seeds of Contemplation.* New Directions, 1949.

Herzensbildung

The Germans have a term that I love, *herzensbildung,* which in English roughly means, "the training of one's heart to see the humanity in another." It's an important concept to consider when thinking about friendship. We only truly connect with each other when our hearts can set aside our defenses and fears and prejudices to see the humanity of the people who walk into our lives. Friends are precious and essential, and are unfortunately sometimes a rare commodity at certain times in our lives when we need them most.

Several years ago, I was leading a medical society discussion group one evening when someone mentioned a study about friendship. As I recall, it said something about the average number of friends people claim in a survey period. We found this problematic for several reasons, in part because people have different kinds of friends. Commonly listed categories include: acquaintances, casual friends, close friends, intimate friends. The last category, the ones we know and who know us inside and out, are the ones that make all the difference.

In his latest book, *How to Know a Person: The Art of Seeing Others Deeply and Being Deeply Seen*, David Brooks examines what it takes to come to know and be known in this way. Brooks shares scary statistics that lend urgency to learning these skills, including that 54% of adults say no one knows them well, and the percentage of people who have no close friends has quadrupled in recent decades. Brooks' thesis is that individually and as a society, we have lost our ability to form "deep" relationships in which we know each other on a level that humans need to feel connected and heard. This type of relationship is not achieved without intentional and informed effort: generous listening, curiosity, "accompaniment," other skills he outlines. There is equal and reciprocal benefit of knowing and being known deeply that can be life changing: "Seeing someone well is a powerfully creative act, no one can fully appreciate their own beauty and strengths unless those things are mirrored back to them in the mind of another."

Brooks writes about two distinct types of people: diminishers and illuminators. Illuminators are capable, even equipped, to see through the superficial—to listen, inquire, and accompany people in a way that leads to deep understanding, encouragement, and illumination, that they in turn mirror back. Illuminators come to understand the depth of your pain and challenges, but also to see and celebrate your unique humanity and worth, your triumphs, and the gifts that you bring to the world around you that others, perhaps even you, may not recognize. As Brooks describes, "They are people who are just curious about you, and they make you feel lit up." He notes that diminishers exist in any group of people, and their behaviors make others feel ignored, stereotyped, and not accepted. He holds that recipients of this treatment who lack close connection with others often lash out against people around them in violent or otherwise vicious ways that are all too common in our society today.

Brooks notes that from the first time you meet illuminators, it is evident that they have the skills to indicate they see you rather than see through you. They make eye contact, they listen, "lean-in listening" he calls it. Importantly, they are instantly curious about you and ask you questions. With nurturing, this leads to a relationship of accompaniment—in a sense just hanging out with an ongoing curiosity that may evolve into a sense of journey together, and a deep sense of understanding and connection.

It was not until well into middle age that I discovered the power of this and the stark contrast that exists between one kind of friendship and another. Three seminal events in my life—my time in seminary, a chance leadership training program in a remote village in Ohio as we launched our physician counseling program, and a long pilgrimage through Spain—all showed me the power of seeing and being seen deeply. This gifted me with new, unexpected, and life-changing friendships, but also with new perspective or direction in other relationships. I'm a slow learner, but better late than never. This unique sense of connection and interconnection is among the most powerful things we can hope for in life, an antidote for much of what ails far too many people. It is, in essence, the way to find ourselves truly accompanied by fellow travelers on our uncertain and winding pilgrimage through life.

Suggested Reading

Books

Brooks, David. *How to Know a Person: The Art of Seeing Others Deeply and Being Deeply Seen.* Random House, 2023.

The Fourfold Path: Telling the Story

Storytelling is a basic human need. Ancient civilizations, Native American cultures, medieval societies with largely illiterate populations—all counted on perpetual, collective storytelling to give cohesion and a sense of heritage to their society. History is now recorded differently, but the need for storytelling is still something that we all crave, something that connects us. Storytelling is important for our mental health. Effective processing and healing from stressful or traumatic events, from mistakes or regret, for repentance, for the giving and receiving of forgiveness, all require us to be willing to tell our story and for there to be a sympathetic and informed listener. Many times we have someone we love and trust to tell our story to, but not everyone has that listener they feel comfortable with, and for them, counseling in its many forms can be life changing.

Not long after we started our counseling program in 2017, we received an evaluation from a colleague who had accessed the program. They noted, "My sessions are incredible. I started therapy because I felt lost and frustrated . . . now I find that the anxiety and fear that held me back are rooted in past experiences that I was never able to unpack . . . Talking about these parts of my life reveals patterns in my behavior. I feel like a massive transformation is taking place . . ."

Among other things, what I believe our colleagues often describe involves both discovering and telling an untold, difficult story, naming the hurts that lie within that story and, in the end, writing an entirely new story. It was a great blessing to read this testimonial and coincidentally came at a time that I was reading the Archbishop Desmond Tutu's *The Book of Forgiving*. In this book, which contains life-changing lessons, Tutu describes the path to forgiveness using the "Fourfold Path." In the often long, complicated, and liberating road to forgiveness of self or others, the four components described in his book are: telling the story, naming the hurt, granting forgiveness, renewing or releasing the relationship.

Telling the story is a critical first step on the road to forgiveness or recovery from trauma. Not just telling yourself the story, but literally telling it out loud to others, to trusted friends, colleagues, family members, or a counselor. Importantly, it involves telling the story several times as retelling the story gradually reveals detail and perspective, clarifies facts, and makes feelings related to the event more tangible and easier to deal with. Tutu notes, "It is not always easy emotionally to take the first step . . . But when we lock our stories inside of us, the initial injury is often compounded."

One of the most important things we can do for each other is to be approachable and available to hear these stories, even when they are difficult to tell and to hear. Our colleagues and friends often have stories to tell about a bad outcome with a patient, a conflict with a colleague, a troubled marriage, perhaps even life-altering depression. Such conversations, especially among men, seldom occur spontaneously, but rather in an atmosphere of safety and trust. They often begin with a simple, but courageous question about whether something is troubling them. The act of checking in with a colleague is an expression of love, and it is telling them that they matter. Many of our colleagues have carried a terrible weight for months, even years, afraid or ashamed to share their very personal stories. Whether they knew it or not, their souls cry out for a chance to tell their stories, to name the hurt, and to begin the process toward healing, the process of releasing the past. Tutu notes that we cannot avoid suffering and trauma in life, but what we can choose is how we will respond, ". . . whether we will let this suffering embitter us or ennoble us. How do we allow our suffering to ennoble us? We make meaning out of it and make it matter."

In each of our lives there are times of great joy, of love, family, friendships, and meaning. Just as surely, life inevitably brings challenges and times of suffering, times that require us to tell our story in order to reclaim wholeness. When I was too young to understand, my family suffered from my father's alcoholism and untimely death caused by it. Looking back, I can see how it negatively influenced my life. Through telling the story of my adolescence, I was able to forgive him and those around him who I assumed had failed him. My college roommate, on the brink of a promising life, was lost to suicide; it was not until well into middle age, having finally told the story during my years in seminary, that I was able to forgive myself and forgive him. As Tutu notes, "We are not responsible for what breaks us, but we can be responsible for what puts us back together again . . . how we begin to repair our broken parts." So much wasted suffering in those years until I was able to release the past, finally able to tell a new story, to turn it into something with meaning, to find a place for it in my heart. For those of you who are in need, I wish the same for you.

Suggested Reading

Books

Tutu, Desmond, and Mpho Tutu. *Book of Forgiving: The Fourfold Path for Healing Ourselves and Our World.* HarperOne, 2014.

A Flight to Nowhere

Evolved as we are, perhaps the ancients have something on us when it comes to the importance of down time. They seemed to recognize that rest and reflection need to be part of the normal cycle of life. Through the millennia, virtually all faith traditions recognized the need to regularly set aside time to catch our breath and get a little perspective, perhaps even a little peace. Even God, busy as He was creating a universe, found time to rest. The religious Sabbath tends to be less faithfully followed these days. Though the roots of the word itself have deeply religious context, "secular sabbath" is written about more and more these days. Its importance in spiritual health is no less vital than for those who practice religious Sabbath. The unbroken frenzy of our lives, working too much, sleeping too little, worrying about our children—and constantly, constantly being plugged in and immediately accessible—creates an internal stew of unrelenting stress hormones that we know is measurably unhealthy but seem powerless to turn off, even temporarily.

So, how might we consider sabbath, secular or otherwise? What sets it apart from the occasional vacation or a few random hours stolen to read, exercise, or watch TV? Most importantly, sabbath is a planned and intentional part of our lives and as a practice, it carries enough importance and commitment to become permanently woven into the fabric of our lives. It is "time set apart"—separated from the daily frenzy that is so often also full of problems and urgency. It can take many forms, but it certainly means being away from work, away from chores, from solving other people's problems, and to some significant extent, to be unplugged. Time to think and reboot, if only temporarily. It might be regular meditation, prayer, exercise, reading, a regularly scheduled "me" day, a round of golf with friends, a long bath at the end of the day, or a favorite walking trail frequently visited. But as a regular, intentional practice, what is the common thread?

Perhaps the real benefit of sabbath comes

down to relationships. When we find time to intentionally step back from work and the electronic hum that has become the unfortunate music of our lives, what we come home to is relationships. In whatever form it takes for you, sabbath should be time and space to reconnect with people you care about and who care about you. Sabbath can be a time and space that allows us to renew and re-explore our relationship with ourselves, and perhaps in looking inward have a chance to connect with something beyond ourselves. The relative stillness we give to ourselves brings about an almost automatic awareness of the undercurrents of our lives that need acknowledgement and with that, hopefully acceptance, change, or gratitude as we set them aside or embrace them.

Sabbath is about finding times of stillness and being open to what that stillness might reveal. Pico Iyer writes of this in *The Art of Stillness* and describes this type of time set apart as "the adventure of going nowhere." In his short book, Iyer, a travel author, ironically makes the case for the importance and accessibility of traveling into your own soul as a preferred destination. He writes, ". . . in an age of constant motion, nothing is more urgent than sitting still. You can go on vacation to Paris or Hawaii... and you'll have a tremendous time, I'm sure. But if you want to come back feeling new—alive and full of fresh hope and in love with the world—I think the place to visit may be nowhere." It is worth the effort. *You* are worth the effort. There is still time. This is your final boarding call... for your flight to nowhere.

Suggested Reading

Books

Iyer, Pico. *The Art of Stillness: Adventures in Going Nowhere.* Simon & Schuster, 2014.

Keating, Thomas. *The Human Condition: Contemplation and Transformation.* Paulist Press, 1999.

Wabi-Sabi

Barely after Halloween, stores fill with Christmas decorations and urgent holiday music. It seems to start earlier each year. Examples of the perfect family, the perfect meal, and beautifully wrapped gifts are everywhere. We start planning and remembering so many wonderful things we look forward to during the holidays. In a way, it really all comes down to celebrating relationships: with people we care about, with ideas, faith, and memories that we treasure. But for some, the holidays can bring sadness or loneliness, a sense of not being enough, a sense of disappointment that the perfect holiday season they had in mind becomes, well . . . imperfect.

Maybe preparing ourselves for holiday and other celebrations should include reconsidering perfection. Rachel Naomi Remen wrote a piece that I always think about that time of year. She notes that while perfectionism is common in our culture, ancient cultures steeped in wisdom found peace by accepting, even celebrating, imperfection. In timeless Japanese culture, Zen gardeners included a misplaced dandelion in the middle of their "perfect" meditation garden and this same culture embraces *wabi-sabi*, a worldview centered on the acceptance of the transience and imperfections of life. *Wabi-sabi* stresses simplicity, modesty, humility, intimacy, and appreciation of the natural world. Native Americans wove a broken "spirit bead" into their intricate beaded costumes, and Puritan quiltmakers left a tiny stain of their own blood in their finished work, acknowledging that art, like human existence, is both imperfect and sacred. As Remen notes, "Nothing with a soul is perfect. When life weaves a spirit bead into your fabric, you may stumble upon a wholeness greater than you had dreamed possible before."

Whether we can pull it off or not, we all know the importance of accepting of our personal imperfections and the imperfections that are inherent in dealing with people, with mystery, with complex diseases. But in day-to-day practice, there is great tension between that and what was drilled into us for years—that when it comes to their health, people expect perfection from us and we were tacitly taught to expect it from ourselves. Coming to terms with this tension and guiding our patients to have some sense of it is a vital ingredient in the doctor-patient relationship. Addressing it with our patients requires humility and honesty on our part. Their accepting takes time and trust on theirs.

Whether we are successful or not with accepting our human imperfections while practicing medicine, accepting it in our lives outside of medicine is more difficult for us as well. That deeply ingrained admonition to not be wrong and to not make stupid mistakes doesn't disappear when we leave the hospital. We are often too slow to admit mistakes, to apologize, to laugh at ourselves, and worst of all, too slow to admit when we are wrong in relationships and work to repair them. Physician divorce rates are evidence enough.

I recently finished Elizabeth Strout's Pulitzer winning novel, *Olive Kitteridge*, a series of stories about an unusually cranky, cynical older woman who becomes a widow and gradually realizes her need for human connection. She reluctantly, but irresistibly, develops a romantic relationship with a man who somehow sees the good in her. She finds herself in unfamiliar territory accepting, even loving, a human in whom she sees many flaws. In the book's closing lines lies a lesson for us all. Strout writes, "And so, if this man next to her was not the man she would have chosen before this time, what did it matter? But here they were, and Olive pictured two slices of Swiss cheese pressed together, such holes they brought to this union-the pieces life took out of you." It's an interesting image, two pieces of Swiss cheese being placed together, the holes and imperfections in each flawed piece covered when brought together. As Jerry Maguire might say, two friends or lovers, or even a doctor and a patient, complete each other when they are finally able to find it in themselves to allow such a thing to happen-to literally embrace imperfection, even when the stakes are high.

Suggested Reading

Books

Remen, Rachel Naomi. *My Grandfather's Blessings: Stories of Strength, Refuge and Belonging.* Riverhead Books, 2001.

Strout. Elizabeth. *Olive Kitteridge.* Random House, 2008.

Song Lyrics

Van Morrison. "These are the Days." *Avalon Sunset,* Mercury, 1989.

The Junk Drawer

It started as a simple repair job. A couple of wooden planks of siding showed signs of rot outside of our kitchen. I called a trusted contractor. Replace a couple of planks, match the paint, and a couple hundred bucks later all should be fine. Right? Well, it's a ninety-year-old house and it is never that simple. The three-month odyssey that ensued involved lifting that whole side of the house, replacing major support beams which in turn stressed our entire kitchen, cracked granite counters, affected plumbing, etc. etc. In the end, what started as a simple carpentry job ended with major renovations. I finally had to bar the contractor from exploring the crawlspace any further. There is just no logical end to what additional horrors he might find. Most of these painful repairs and improvements are entirely invisible, unless one were to extensively army-crawl under the house to inspect the magnificent new beams that adorn the crawlspace.

Weeks later, most of the nightmare and clutter were behind us except for one very visible remnant. Purposely placed in a room we seldom inhabit, it sits on an ottoman in the living room, far enough away that I don't have to deal with it. However, it still catches my eye as I pass by, taunting me. Yes, it is the kitchen junk drawer, displaced during the renovation, its mother cabinet now resting in demo heaven. It is an orphan now, wanting attention, and it is no longer easy to ignore.

Every household has at least one junk drawer, and I'm betting you have more than one. This is where we toss the things that were once necessary, but now we don't quite know what to do with them. I mean, they might be necessary, perhaps even essential someday, but in my heart, I know . . . probably not. But maybe. I've glanced several times, even discarded about half of it late one night, but it's a bottomless pit. Batteries (used?), a dozen keys to locks that probably don't still exist . . . but might. Hair clips we used to put in our daughters' hair as they ate breakfast or as we hurried out the door almost late for school. Bread wrapper twisties, super glue in various states of decay, and on and on. A drawer full of things I don't want to deal with.

Why am I still thinking, even writing, about this? My preoccupation with what still lurks in the crawlspace is well founded, I think. But also, I'm reminded of past readings about Carl Jung and our shadow—that archetypal figure that lives in the unconscious and possesses the parts of ourselves we don't want to acknowledge, something writers often describe as lurking in our subconscious basement or under the bed. Perhaps, but in this case, I think it has more to do with ninety-year-old wiring I don't want to confront rather than my shadow, though both could probably use some attention.

The junk drawer? Just Google the psychology of that. There are countless articles, blogs, images, videos, even entire books exploring this. As author Jeremy Berg notes of junk drawers, "We do something similar with our spiritual life. We are constantly accumulating feelings, experiences, wounds, doubts, conflicts, and questions, and we don't quite know where to put them. Many of these don't fit into our preferred life script, and so they begin piling up in some deep and hidden place in our soul." More poetically, Poetic Father noted,

> The mind must be Cleansed
> From time to time
> That is how your dreams
> have room to grow.

It's a lovely poem, but it requires two difficult things, both reminiscent of what happens when the junk drawer is finally cleaned out and then repurposed for something more useful. First, it requires deliberate discernment, an honest appraisal of what in our lives has hijacked our thoughts, our precious hours, and filled them with junk. What is this junk that has accumulated, crowding out things that are more nourishing, things that our soul yearns for? Second, it requires that we rediscover our deepest dreams, our better angels, our sense of things that really matter. That's what goes in the drawer. Organizing and filling it, that is the work of a lifetime, the footprints of a life well-lived.

Suggested Reading

Articles

Berg, Jeremy. "Junk Drawer Spirituality (Huddle Qs)." *Kingdom Harbor,* 2 Dec. 2019. https://kingdomharbor.com/2019/12/02/junk-drawer-faith-huddle-qs/.

Poetry

Poetic Father. "Junk Drawer." *All Poetry,* 2016.

IN THE WILDERNESS

The Space Between the Notes

For most of my life, I've wanted to learn to play a musical instrument. When I was young, I took lessons trying out all kinds of instruments: guitar, piano, drums, violin. I even resorted to the ukulele, and my elementary school music teacher stayed after school for several sessions until we both gave it up as hopeless. There is just something missing in my wiring that even practice and some measure of perseverance couldn't overcome. In midlife, one Sunday after being especially touched by our church pianist's rendition of "One Bread, One Body," I tried teaching myself to play just that one song on our piano (yes, we have a piano that taunts me as I pass by it every day). I pounded out those notes at night for weeks, trying to force-teach myself just one song. In the end, I decided it was much like trying to teach a monkey to play the piano, perhaps even less successful than that, and I finally gave up.

I recall a comment that my guitar teacher made well into my year as a wannabe Beatle in sixth grade. He said something to the effect of, "Anybody can finger the notes. That comes from your brain, but the rhythm has to come from your heart." It came to mind again recently when I read the famous quote from the French composer Claude Debussy: "Music is the space between the notes."

We all have colleagues whom we greatly admire, and when we think about them, they are seldom primarily defined by superior intellect. They are usually not the smartest person in the room, but often they are the kindest person in the room. They intuitively know the important rhythms of life and the important rhythms of practicing medicine. They know the notes as well as anyone. Perhaps more importantly, they know where to put the pauses, both when they are treating patients, but also within their lives outside of medicine with the people they love.

What defines us, both within and beyond

our lives in medicine? Perhaps it's a combination of the people and things we have faith in-things that we value above all else, but also it's the expressions of our souls that are visible to those around us-the songs that our lives sing. What often causes physician distress is when we are just banging out the notes day after day, ignoring the importance of the pauses, the importance of acknowledging and savoring the rhythms of life that we are meant to live, even at work. If we listen closely enough, within the space between the notes in our lives. we can discover a hidden wholeness, a rhythm that makes our lives not just a series of notes, but a sacred song.

Suggested Reading

Books

Palmer, Parker. *A Hidden Wholeness: The Journey Toward an Undivided Life*. Jossey-Bass, 2004.

Poetry

Hughes, Langston. "Dreams." *The Dream Keeper and Other Poems*, Alfred A. Knopf, 1932.

Extroverts, Tortured Poets, and the Long Journey

Arthur Brooks is a Harvard researcher and writer who has made it his mission in life to define and study happiness. He collaborated with Oprah Winfrey to write *Build the Life You Want: The Art and Science of Getting Happier*. It is an interesting read, but if I'm honest, after several years of reading increasingly complex research on basic concepts like happiness, gratitude, generosity, forgiveness, self-compassion, and the like, I'm starting to feel that when detailed, "scientific" research is applied to these basic traits of the heart, they often lose some of their spiritual gravitas.

Among other topics, Brooks and Winfrey take a close look at personality types and how happiness might be influenced by our tendency to be extroverts or introverts. Using scales to categorize people into extrovert vs. introvert and happy vs. unhappy, four categories emerge: happy extroverts, unhappy extroverts, happy introverts, and unhappy introverts (tortured poets). As a group, extroverts are twice as likely to be happy, but fortunately for us introverts, there are caveats. He notes that extroverts tend to have more friends, but often most of these are casual or transactional friends. They have a tendency to have few close friends in whom they confide and connect deeply with, whereas many introverts are happy because even though they have fewer friends, the relationships they gravitate to and maintain are often deeply nourishing.

The book was a timely read for me, digesting it as I attended a 50th high school reunion. Having just read a book about happiness, would I reach any conclusions about my old classmates and how life, gray hair, and waning hormones have changed them? Looking back on my own time in high school, with the added perspective as an observer of my own children and their friends in those years, I realize that we each have our own unique perception of those formative years. Some of us were perfectly miserable, and a few of us arguably experienced the pinnacle of our lives in high school. For most of us, the memories are mostly good, but within the parentheses of those years lie some regrets that are painful still. More often than not, they are regrets about how we treated each other in ways hard to understand decades later.

My family moved when I was in high school, and this year, there are two reunions for me. In my first high school with my childhood friends, I was an introvert, a pensive, petulant kid who spent most of those first two years daydreaming and getting in trouble. In the remote, rural high school where I spent my junior and senior years, I accidentally reinvented myself, quickly developed friends, and became class president. True to Brooks' description, the friends I am close with to this day are those from my introvert years, and I have mostly lost contact with friends from my second high school where my friendships were a mile wide and an inch deep.

I didn't reach any conclusions about happiness as, like deciphering other people's marriages, the casual assessment of someone else's happiness can be deceiving. What stood out most of all at the reunion was that the lines of high school hierarchy and the dreaded cliques had disappeared. There was easy, relaxed, jovial conversation and openness that crossed all these lines as if they had never existed.

At one of the events, I stood outside the bar where we gathered, finishing a phone call, when someone from the old days walked up, someone I rarely interacted with back then, even though we saw each other daily. We visited for a minute when unexpectedly they teared up and told me they had lost a sibling unexpectedly just a few days earlier. We stood there and hugged—embraced really—something that would have been unimaginable all those years ago. Yet it seemed so natural now, the winding road we had traveled leading us to a common destination. It reminded me of a line from the movie *Almost Famous*, when the main character laments about being marginalized in high school. His older mentor reassures him, "You'll meet them all again on their long journey to the middle."

Suggested Reading

Books

Brooks, Arthur, and Oprah Winfrey. *Build the Life you Want: The Art and Science of Getting Happier.* Portfolio, 2023.

Movies

Crowe, Cameron, director. *Almost Famous.* DreamWorks, 2000.

Poetry

Adcock, Gary. "The Reunion." *All Poetry,* 2023.

A View From Section 5

Just as surely as "politics spoils a party," talking politics spoils a medical office visit. The last few years during the Trump-Biden-Trump era when things were particularly nasty, I did my best to divert any conversation with patients away from political discussion. It's always been interesting how long-time patients that I know well and love just assume that I think exactly like they do, regardless of what their particular political passions might be. It's best just to shake my head, smile, and change the subject. Still, as much as I would like the office to be a sanctuary from it, some patients just won't let it go. Sometimes I have my own anxiety from it, sometimes even anger, and while I like to be well-informed, watching the news lately makes me mad ... or sad, as do "casual conversations" about it with patients. Like many of you, regardless of your political leanings, it often makes me wonder how our country can survive the meanness and division.

But there was this one night in the fall of 2024 that, at least for the moment, set me right. It was pretty close to a perfect night with my son and granddaughters at the Texas–Georgia football game. The temperature was in the seventies with a little breeze blowing in at dusk, finally seeming a little like fall. The crowd was loud and excitement was reaching a fevered pitch when the national anthem started. Suddenly, 100,000 people had their hands or hats on their hearts and sang together. It's always been an emotional moment at UT games for me and often I tear up a little, but that night, it was much more—what some theologians might call a unitive experience. A tingle up my spine and a sense of being lifted up, momentarily inhabiting a thin space that separates the world from the soul and the unseen beyond, an intense sense of connection. With perfect timing, as we sang the last few lines, two B-1 bombers flew over the stadium, incredibly low, loud, and powerful, blazing off to the south silhouetted by the fading blue sky and pink clouds of the sunset, their afterburners blasting fire with a furious roar punctuating the moment. I must admit that this time around I more than teared up. It was just such an incredible experience, all those people united in a common expression of patriotism. In that moment, as Americans, we were at our best.

The unitive, or mystical, experience is sometimes described as a sudden, spontaneous, intensely deep and emotional sense of unity or oneness going beyond our usual sensory and cognitive understanding. Well, I'm no mystic, but for me, I'd describe it as a fleeting moment being lifted up by intense connection, both with all that is around me and all that is beyond. I've felt it a handful of other times I can easily recall: when I held my first grandchild, when I saw my bride poised at the entrance of the sanctuary, framed from behind with the afternoon sun pouring into the narthex all those years ago, when I stood on a cliff at Finisterre overlooking the endless sea at the end of a long pilgrimage through Spain. Those were equally powerful, but somehow more explainable. So why at a football game?

The game took place in that particularly contentious season of American history, sometimes seemingly defined by suspicion, disrespect, and meanness. But in the end, there is much more good than bad around us, and in that moment, shoulder-to-shoulder with all those strangers, those differences faded for a brief instant. The divine spark, the essence of transcendent humanity present in us all, seemed possible again. It was a sense of what author Gregory Boyle calls our "unshakeable goodness," the notion that within us all there is a diamond, "often covered with dust," but it is there nonetheless. Our great calling and hope is to look for that in everyone and no matter how hard it seems at times, not to give up on each other. Standing there that night singing together, it somehow reminded me of going arm-in-arm with my colleagues all these years, through so many challenges, saves, and joys.

One of the many things that makes me proud of our physician family is how though we are smart people with strong, varied opinions, for the most part we stay above the fray of political malevolence with each other. Politics only occasionally comes up with colleagues during my daily lunch at the hospital, and when it does, I've never experienced any tension in those discussions. Most of the time, there is an unspoken but palpable sense of respect and admiration for each other when we gather and share our thoughts and stories in the doctor's dining room or hallways at the hospital.

It's unlikely that any of us sensed a mystical experience when we filled out our ballots in that election cycle; but one of the great practices of wellness is gratitude. We can practice gratitude by being aware of the things that we have been given, things that we have been blessed with, and to acknowledge that they are just gifts. Fleeting though many of those gifts are, some endure. Hopefully, something that endures is our love of country, regardless of whom we vote for, and the opportunities and freedoms that we are blessed with here. At times it is as much a hope and an idea as it is a reality, but there is a reason why when we stand to sing our national anthem, we put our hands over our hearts, and for a moment we are all as one.

Suggested Reading

Poetry

Bates, Katherine Lee. "America the Beautiful." *The Congregationalist*, 4 July 1895.

Regret

The doctor's dining room was eerily quiet as I was having lunch with a colleague at the hospital a few months into the COVID-19 pandemic shutdown. We barely know each other but saw each other frequently, and we just happened to be in the dining room at the same time. Both hungry for conversation with a human with masks off, we sat down a few feet apart and ate lunch. In the spring of 2020, everyone was hypervigilant about getting infected. The hospital was not risking a serving line with hot food or a salad bar, but rather a bleak selection of wrapped sandwiches or salads packed tightly in small plastic cubes. Most of the doctors had stopped eating there, just passing through to frown over the food and grab a bag of chips to eat on the run, so we had the room to ourselves.

My new friend spent their days in the hospital, trying to deliver good care under very difficult conditions. A couple of weeks earlier, they had received a call from their sister in another city. Their brother-in-law had contracted COVID, in those very scary early days of the Delta strain. He was an otherwise healthy man, but well into his sixties. They talked to their brother-in-law, and he sounded fine, not short of breath, a rare cough, body aches, and a low grade fever. My friend advised his sister that she keep him at home unless he got much sicker, as the hospital was no place to be right then if it could be avoided.

That night, he became acutely short of breath and was in full cardiopulmonary arrest when EMS arrived. He passed away in the ER with a massive heart attack. My colleague was devastated, ashamed, and racked with guilt, though it is doubtful their brother-in-law would have been admitted with his mild symptoms earlier even if they had advised him differently. There was really no consoling them at that point, and I doubt they have ever gotten over it. A seemingly minor fork in the road that day would take an emotional toll for years.

As I reflected on their story, I was reminded what a powerful burden regret can be. It can be a cloud that follows us, hangs over us, for days ... often for years. Regret feels bad because it comes with a sense of personal failure, is often visible to those around us, and is accompanied by self-blame, shame, and sometimes guilt. Studies show that regret is a common emotion, and 70% of adults have a significant sense of regret. While those studies demonstrate the most common sources of regret involve education, career, romance, and parenting, I've found with physicians who seek support that their regrets involve relationships, career choices, medical mistakes, choices related to alcohol or substance abuse, or choices that adversely impact work-life integration. Researchers point out that regret related to inaction is more difficult to navigate than regret related to choices that turned out badly, because the possibilities with the former are almost limitless, as opposed to the more concrete consequences of the latter.

Regret can fester because left in isolation we often tend to dwell on it. As Amy Summerville describes, "We develop the reflex to chew and chew on an unfortunate turn of events, like a cow on its cud, till there is no nutrition left in it." This can be paralyzing when major, life-altering events occur that involve regret unless we reframe regret into something constructive.

All major religions and spiritual belief systems share a common theme that author Richard Rohr describes as the order → disorder → reorder cycle. Traditional Native American cultures use metaphoric cycles of day-night-sunrise or the order of seasons. World mythologies consistently tell stories in a journey-fall-return to a new home pattern. Recovery programs explore innocence-addiction-recovery, while Christianity centers around life-death-resurrection. The list is endless, but the point is the same. In any life, chances are we will, at some point, encounter what mystics called the "dark night of the soul"—a crossroads, with regret often a prominent feature, a place from which with some effort, we might emerge into a new life that has not only escaped the bonds of regret, but has acquired wisdom from it. Rohr notes that even in distress, we attempt to avoid the hard work of real change, the orderly progression from disorder to reorder. We often attempt to "jump from stage I to stage III" of this common cycle, bypassing the personal growth that comes from confronting regret.

The liminal space between disorder and reorder is often described as a wilderness, a time of disorientation and unsure footing where the pathway out may be obscure. Discovery of that path is deeply personal and requires naming and confronting regret. It means being open to accepting support from family, friends, counselors, pastors, or colleagues, many of whom probably inhabited that same space at some point. It requires looking inward, self-compassion, a sense of hope and, perhaps the hardest part of all, patience. While in the wilderness, if we look closely, we may find angels that were sent to protect us, sometimes in the most unexpected places.

Author David Whyte sums it up well, "Sincere regret may in fact be a faculty for paying attention to the future, for sensing a new tide where we missed a previous one . . . regret turns our eyes, attentive and alert, to a future possibly lived better than our past." Painful and lasting as it can be, regret is a springboard for personal growth, for renewed relationships, and a source of wisdom gained from pain, but only if it is fully told, confronted, put into perspective, then tucked away. Sometimes it is hard to convince ourselves that we are all human, we all make mistakes, when we wish we could change our past. In its worst forms, it is hard to overcome without help, without love and human connection that helps us in our darkest hours.

Suggested Reading

Articles

Grierson, Bruce. "The Meaning of Regret." *Psychology Today,* 31 Oct. 2017, https://www.psychologytoday.com/us/blog/the-carpe-diem-project/201710/the-meaning-regret.

Books

Brueggemann, Walter. *Spirituality of the Psalms (Facets).* Fortress Press, 2001.

Rohr, Richard. *The Wisdom Pattern: Order, Disorder, Reorder.* Franciscan Media, 2020.

Whyte, David. "Regret." *Consolations: The Solace, Nourishment and Underlying Meaning of Everyday Words,* Many Rivers Press, 2021.

Poetry

Bush-Banks, Olivia Ward. "Regret." *Poets.org*.

Masters, Edgar Lee. "George Gray." *Spoon River Anthology*, Macmillan, 1915.

Song Lyrics

Buffett, Jimmy. "A Pirate Looks at Forty." *A1A*, ABC/Dunhill Records, 1974.

The Antidote to Shame

Just hearing the word shame carries weight. It brings up bad memories. Shame is a powerful emotion that results when we believe we haven't lived up to expectations and values or otherwise deviated from social norms. Shame is often a deep, lasting emotion occurring as a consequence of a misstep that is visible to those around us. It can lead to a perception that we have failed others or are inept, inconsiderate, or careless in our actions. It can lead to all kinds of maladaptive internal and external responses. Shame is particularly painful in medicine, where so much of our professional identities are tied up in not making mistakes or being involved in a bad outcome.

Shame is a common emotion. As I was putting together this essay, I discussed it with a colleague who also likes to write as we ate lunch one day ... just how hard it is to really capture what shame feels like in writing. They suggested I read the book *In the Heart of the Sea: The Tragedy of the Whaleship Essex* by Nathaniel Philbrick. It tells the true story of the sinking of the Essex, an early 19th century whaler that sailed out of Nantucket only to sink after being attacked repeatedly by a huge whale on open sea. Only a few survived after three months at sea in small lifeboats, enduring exposure, thirst, and cannibalism. They were eventually rescued 3,000 miles away off the coast of Chile. The captain survived and returned to Nantucket, the fantastic story of the whale attack confirmed but his role in it still suspect. He went to sea once more, and his next ship hit a coral reef and sunk. No longer employable as a captain, he lived out his days in obscurity as a night watchman.

So powerful was the story and the captain's shame that Herman Melville wrote *Moby Dick* based on these events. He had met the beached captain and remarked, "To the islanders he was a nobody. To me, the most impressive man, tho' wholly unassuming, even humble . . ." As I finished the book, I could only imagine the shame he must have endured, and I wondered if anyone cared. I've never lost a whaleship, but in our work, we too are captains of a ship, and like most, I've felt the burden of shame often enough in medical training and beyond.

We traded stories of shame that day at lunch, at least the ones we were willing to tell. I remembered that during my residency in the 1980s, still learning, I stopped a patient's chronic steroids far too abruptly, leading to hypotension and a cardiac event. He recovered, but barely, and the case was presented at a weekly mortality and morbidity conference, logarithmically compounding my sense of failure and shame. To this day, the memory is incredibly painful.

Almost two decades ago, I heard Brené Brown speak at my daughter's high school. It was before I was familiar with her work. A line from her talk did stick and I've thought about it many times since, especially in interactions with physicians experiencing distress or addictive behavior. I couldn't recall the exact wording until I came across it recently: "Everyone has a story or a struggle that will break your heart. And, if we're really paying attention, most people have a story that will bring us to our knees." For the most part, those struggles, often involving shame, are mostly hidden from view, even when carried by people we think we know pretty well, smoldering and informing their behavior and mental well-being.

While guilt is a sense that "I *did* something bad," shame is a sense that "I *am* bad," and Brown describes it as "the swampland of the soul." When shame is unaddressed, it can cause despair that fuels destructive behavior, addiction, and a variety of mental health issues. Brown points out that shame expresses itself differently in men and women. In men, shame stems from the fear of being perceived as weak, while in, women it's a sense of failing to live up to the complex web of expectations society lays on them. Beyond that, physicians in general are susceptible to shame, born of subtle indoctrination in training and early career to deny imperfections.

Brown writes, "Empathy is the antidote to shame." Like shame, empathy is a hot topic these days and has as many definitions as it does researchers. A basic definition would be "the ability to understand and share the feelings of another." Empathy requires genuine caring, generous listening, and the life experiences that we bring to a relationship and are willing to share. It can be the foundation of a deep, sometimes life-changing relationship with profound trust. Empathy has the power to transform shame.

Mother Teresa once said, "If I look at the mass, I will never act. If I look at the one, I will." Within the family of medicine, we are meant to look out for each other actively, tangibly, and in ways that the institutions we inhabit can't or won't. From 30,000 feet, it seems an overwhelming task, but on the ground, one colleague at a time, it is entirely within our power to make a difference. We check in. We give space for the people we work with and care about to confide, to connect. When needed, we accept or ask for the same for ourselves. So many of our colleagues, even those we know well, have hidden trauma or distress that they try to muscle through in silence. Their suffering will remain hidden unless we are standing face-to-face with them, paying attention, and taking the time to recognize it.

Suggested Reading

Books

Brown, Brené. *I Thought It Was Just Me: Women Reclaiming Power and Courage in a Culture of Shame.* Gotham, 2007.

Philbrick, Nathaniel. *In the Heart of the Sea, the Sinking of the Whaleship Essex*. Penguin, 2001.

Poetry

Angelou, Maya. "Still I Rise." *And Still I Rise*, Random House, 1978.

Scripture

The Bible, *Genesis 3:1-13*

Broken Open

One of the things that defines families or lifelong friends is that while time and circumstance may cause us to drift apart, sudden tragedy or loss brings us back together and reminds us the importance of our connections with loved ones, and how difficult it is to face life's storms alone. One terrible week, still in those strange, dark days of the pandemic, our local medical community stood witness to an unspeakable tragedy—the random and violent death of one of our colleagues. She was a young, truly beloved member of our medical family: a wife, mother, caring doctor, lover of Mardi Gras. She had an infectious laugh and sense of humor and energy. The loss was so sudden and so awful that virtually the entire community, both those who knew her well and those like me who barely knew her at all, were universally shocked and speechless. There followed a week of vigils and a time when our family of physicians in Austin figuratively, and often literally, reached out to console, hug, encourage, and commiserate over collective loss, and weeks beyond that with Mardi Gras ribbons tied on trees all over our city, mourning our loss.

Around that time, a friend gave me the book *Broken Open* by Elizabeth Lesser. Lesser's book is billed as an "inspiring guide to healing and growth ... even in the face of loss and adversity." I found myself less than fulfilled when I read the book, not that it doesn't have profound truth in it, but rather that it seemed inadequate for the moment. In this and other times of unimaginable tragedy, people often, and rightly so, refer to the stages of grief, our search for meaning, the "Hero's Journey" from mythology, the mystic's "dark night of the soul," scripture, or other profound writings. All of these contain truth, even hope, but in the raw sadness of the moment when we feel lost, it can be difficult to find comfort or any grain of understanding in them.

During the first decade of our local physician wellness, counseling, and recovery programs, our medical family went through this and other times of great trauma—times that shook us to our core, and left our community feeling disoriented and grieving deeply. It is in these times that we question so many things, and we look around us for an anchor, for connection, for any way to make sense of tragedy.

A few years back, a patient of mine was telling me about a hobby of his, a passion really, called *kintsugi* and I thought of him as I tried to make sense of that terrible time. *Kintsugi* is a Japanese artistic practice, and later a philosophy, with origins in the 15th century. Legend has it that the Shogun Ashikaga Yoshimasa always used his favorite bowl for the tea ceremony. The bowl was broken and sent back to China, where a clumsy repair using a rusty staple was eventually returned to him. He instructed his Japanese craftsman to come up with a more aesthetic solution to repairing his cherished bowl and from that, *kintsugi* was born. In this practice, the tiny shards of a broken object are collected, sorted, cleaned, and assembled one by one with meticulous precision. The pieces are precisely glued, then sanded, then the remaining cracks are filled in by successive layers of lacquer, then sprinkled with gold or other precious metal powder. The metal mingles with moist lacquer to give an illusion of flowing metal. The gold "scars" are then burnished, and a new work of art, meticulously created from the original, takes on new life. It is a practice that takes large measures of patience and time, for to rush the process leads to undesirable results rather than a thing of beauty.

They described this hobby during one of those seasons of grief, a time of trying to put our shattered lives back together, something that is in a way the basis of the *kintsugi* philosophy of healing and hope. Even after profound damage, a healing of sorts may take place, but only over time, layer by layer, the shards of damage slowly pieced together, pieces slowly becoming part of the whole again. Though forever changed, it is eventually sealed and burnished, with patience and love, into an entirely new object, a lovely and precious piece of art that makes no attempts to hide its traumatic history, even as we marvel at its beauty.

Suggested Reading

Books

Lesser, Elizabeth. *Broken Open: How Difficult Times Can Help Us Grow.* Villard, 2005.

O'Donohue, John. "Absence, Where Longing Still Lingers." *Eternal Echoes: Celtic Reflections on Our Yearning to Belong,* Harper Perrenial, 2000.

Poetry

Frost, Robert. "Stopping by Woods on a Snowy Evening." *New Hampshire*, Henry Holt and Company, 1923.

A Train in the Distance

When I was around ten years old, my grandparents lived in a tiny town of 300 in rural Texas. In the early 1900s, Lorena was a bustling railroad town, its economy fueled by the cotton industry, with huge cotton gins lined up along the railroad track. By the 1960s, the town was a skeleton of itself; downtown buildings and the cotton gins that were once the heartbeat of the town were now abandoned and falling to ruin. In an era where children were essentially raised free-range, my cousins and I would spend our days exploring and playing in the old buildings. One of my most vivid memories was the trains that went by. When we heard them coming, we would run out of the ruins and stand just a few feet from the tracks to feel the sheer power of them shake our little bodies as the train went by. The conductor would look at us out his open window, so close that we could see his smile and the watch on his wrist. Around the same time, our family went on a memorable, cross-country train trip, boarding the California Zephyr in Denver and riding it all the way to Sacramento. We watched half the country pass by in those few days, one of the great memories from my childhood before my father passed away.

When my own children were around ten years old, we lived in a house in Austin just a block away from the railroad tracks that run through the middle town. Of course, I was more cautious with them, but we would still revisit my childhood, standing at the end of the street as trains passed by. We would occasionally put pennies on the track, then retrieve the flattened, unrecognizable metal after the train passed by. Now my grandchildren see or hear those same trains pass through our town, a familiar sight and sound of their youth as well, though nowadays mostly ignored. My mother is alive and well at 95, and while her parents and the house in Lorena are long gone, she lives in a retirement community just a few hundred yards away from those same railroad tracks in Austin. The trains are audible from the courtyard outside of her apartment, bringing memories of trains that have seemingly been a thread connecting generations in our family.

My wife and I live less than a mile from an active train track that goes through the middle of our town. There's a train that goes by every morning right at 4 a.m., and we hear the faint hum of the train and three long, mournful bellows from its whistle as it passes by. We are up every morning at that time, completing tasks that require doing and repositioning before falling back to sleep.

It has been an adjustment to become a caregiver, but in our house that term needs some clarification. Though my wife needs significant assistance and, unfortunately for her, she is the recipient of my caregiving, in most other ways that really matter, she takes much better care of me than I do for her, so we rarely use the term. Still, it is a challenge for both of us. Her illness has caused us to give up some things from our "before life," and make major adjustments to try and thrive in our new life as it evolves. It requires patience and acceptance, characteristics that don't come naturally to me. Sometimes I need some help reviving a positive outlook, something I have come to realize often requires acceptance.

Acceptance is surprisingly hard to fully define, harder still to describe how to achieve. *The Book of Joy: Lasting Happiness in a Changing World* by the Dalai Lama and Desmond Tutu states, "The Dalai Lama had told us that stress and anxiety come from our expectations of how life should be. When we are able to accept that life is how it is, not as we think it should be, we are able to ease the ride ... with all its suffering, stress, anxiety, and dissatisfaction ..." Acceptance means fully acknowledging the facts of a current situation or circumstance and not fixating on why it should not be that way. The authors go on to note, "Much of traditional Buddhist practice is directed towards the ability to see life accurately, beyond all the expectations, projections, and distortions that we typically bring to it." Acceptance, as a practice, allows us to thoughtfully respond, rather than impulsively react.

Two critical concepts about acceptance should be noted. First, acceptance is often an active, powerful response rather than entirely passive, as it is sometimes misunderstood to be. Acceptance does not mean turning our backs on important issues. In no way does it mean we don't work for change or try to right the wrongs we see. At the same time, many things we accept cannot be changed. Twelve step recovery programs hold both acceptance and thoughtful response for change as core concepts. The very first of the twelve steps is acceptance of being powerless over alcohol. The Serenity Prayer, often evoked at AA meetings, says, "Grant me the serenity to accept the things I cannot change, the courage to change the things I can, and the wisdom to know the difference." Second, acceptance allows us to release the past, to set down disappointments, mistakes, bad luck, or just the realities of the world that led us to our current circumstances, and allows us to respond and look forward.

Psychotherapist Amy Morin suggests a number of strategies for nurturing acceptance in difficult situations. Some of them are:

1. Accept how you feel about a situation. Be honest with yourself about how the situation is affecting you.

2. Stick to the facts. Try to distinguish the situation from all the emotions it has triggered.

3. Accept the situation as a fixed reality. This does not preclude a thoughtful response or solution down the road when you have had a chance to separate the facts from the emotions.

4. Remember that you can still have a good life even with challenges and suffering along the way. Therapists often use a variety of behavioral therapy techniques to help clients who struggle with acceptance.

When we wake each morning at 4 a.m. and hear the train whistle that's close enough to be heard in the quiet, but far enough away that it is deep in the background, I am comforted. It always reminds me of a Paul Simon song, "Train in the Distance." Simon's song suggests that we love the faraway sound of a train as it symbolizes the importance of moving forward, leaving the past behind, of the hope for a better life somewhere down the line. I struggle with acceptance. And so, I try to remind myself, each day (or night) that acceptance of current circumstance—the past set aside—is what keeps us grounded and grateful in the present, allowing us to look forward to the future . . . with hope.

Suggested Reading

Blessings

Bowler, Kate, and Jessica Richie. "A Blessing for the Caregivers." *Good Enough: 40ish Devotions for a Life of Imperfection*, Convergent Books, 2022.

Books

Dalai Lama, and Desmond Tutu. *The Book of Joy: Lasting Happiness in a Changing World.* Avery, 2016.

Morin, Amy. *13 Things Mentally Strong People Don't Do: Take Back Your Power, Embrace Change, Face Your Fears, and Train Your Brain for Happiness and Success.* William Morrow, 2017.

Poetry

Frost, Robert. "Acceptance." *West-Running Brook*, Henry Holt and Company, 1928

Whyte, David. "The Truelove." *The Sea in You: Twenty Poems of Requited and Unrequited Love*, Many Rivers Press, 2015.

Song Lyrics

Simon, Paul. "Train in the Distance." *Hearts and Bones*, Warner Bros. Records, 1983.

Taylor, James. "You Can Close Your Eyes." *Sweet Baby James*, Warner Bros. Records, 1970.

Hope Floats

Coming out of those chaotic pandemic years, most of us had gone through at least some form of reflection or assessment of habits, relationships, and work. It's easy to get caught up, sometimes for years at a time, in routines that deplete us. Sometimes we feel unable to make much-needed steps toward change, only to feel stuck, even helpless. In those years, in our work with physicians in our counseling program, I found great admiration for so many who made much-needed life changes that often went against the institutional culture of medicine and our own bad habits. Change snuck up on me when I realized that I was just terribly inefficient with telemedicine in those early days of the shutdown. Appointment slots were lengthened, which became something I found myself unwilling to undo once I went back to seeing patients in the office.

With a lighter schedule, my days were less

chaotic and stressful, and I came to love my work again. I'm nearer the end than the beginning of my career, my kids are off the payroll, and I'm self-employed. So admittedly, I am able to make changes that not everyone can to make my work more sustainable in the years to come. Still, I have to shake my head that it took me so long to realize that not working myself into the ground is well worth the bottom-line sacrifice. Still, old habits are hard to break and as I eased back on my workload, for a time I felt a certain unease, a sense that I wasn't working hard enough.

To further confound my financial planner, in 2021, in a time of uncertainty and sometimes impulsive moves, we bought a little farm an hour or so from town. It was a steep learning curve of wells and septic fields, irrigation systems and permits, spiders and snakes, but I fell in love with the old farmhouse and the struggling olive grove that had covered much of the property until that terrible freeze. Since then, I've planted new trees and have tended to them like children. It's a metaphor for our own recovery from those terrible first two years of the pandemic, but I'll set that aside for now. Relaxing there and not worrying about patients quickly morphed into worrying about the grove. However, it's a different kind of worry, and there is satisfaction in watching life being breathed back into the place, ever so slowly. I wander and tend to it weekends and have made each of my grandchildren adopt a couple of the struggling trees, measure, and talk to them when they visit.

It's an experience that made me reconsider hope. I can imagine how people who farm or ranch for a living center their lives around hope each year, just as we do when we look at our children, grandchildren, patients, friends, or family members who are struggling or ill, or when we wish our workdays would nourish rather than exhaust us. Hope is the underlying current in optimism, the wind in the sails of our lives, and without it, we are set adrift. Even with all the challenges it brought, those pandemic years gave me a chance to reconsider what I hope for, sometimes pray for, and what I should let go of.

The drive to the grove is about the right distance to unwind and, for the moment at least, leave the worries of work behind. About fifteen miles from my turnoff, I pass by Smithville. There is a sign on the highway announcing "Smithville: Home of *Hope Floats*." It was a popular movie filmed there—a story about humility, divorce, childhood trauma, and death of a loved one, but in the midst of it, from the ashes, a new family, happiness, wisdom, and hope emerge. I watched it again recently, trying to remember the line in the movie that the title comes from. It is at the end when Sandra Bullock's character notes, "Beginnings are scary, endings are usually sad, but it is the middle that counts the most . . . Just give hope a chance to float up, and it will . . ." The sign is badly faded, and whizzing by a bit above the speed limit, all I see each time is the reminder that "Hope Floats." And that is enough.

Suggested Reading

Blessings

Bowler, Kate, and Jessica Richie. "A Blessing for Slowing Down." *Good Enough: 40ish Devotions for a Life of Imperfection*, Convergent Books, 2022.

Movies

Hope Floats. Directed by Forest Whitaker, 20th Century Fox, 1998.

Scripture

The Bible, *Romans 5:3-4*

Miracle Shall Follow Miracle

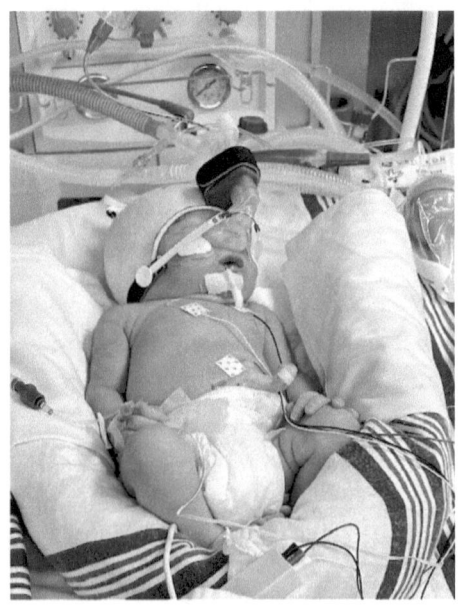

January

The year 2024 started with our eighth grandchild, born too early, struggling in the NICU. It was an extended stay causing all the anxiety and uncertainty you'd expect. Little Brooks struggled with each breath for many days, needing support until his own life force would emerge. We were so blessed with expert care and kindness by everyone in the NICU. And then, almost overnight, Brooks became Brooks . . . and he was ready to go home. So many more things could have gone wrong but didn't. There was expert care to be sure, but still I couldn't help appreciating both the mystery and the miracle that were right there in front of us.

Later in the year, a long-time patient of mine with a complex autoimmune disease struggled for a month in the same hospital, much of that time critically ill, her fate uncertain. She is no stranger to being this ill, but it seemed different this time. I've become very attached to her, and I prayed for her daily and worried about her constantly. She made an amazing recovery, nothing short of miraculous, and there was great mystery involved as to just how she had survived. Why did she survive when others who receive similar levels of care don't?

We are very good at what we do. We control chronic disease, keep people healthy, even save desperately ill patients with some regularity, but in doing so, sometimes I think we give ourselves too much credit, even give science too much credit. Rachel Naomi Remen notes, "We have traded mystery for mastery." We have largely lost the ability to recognize what lies beyond our grasp in treating our patients. We have lost our ability to recognize the great mysteries of life and what goes on beneath the surface of medical care. In the great debate over the value of science in public and private decision making that raged these last few years, perhaps we have sometimes taken it too far. Maybe we allowed ourselves to let science define the very essence of life, to let ourselves take too much credit-or too much blame-for outcomes in the care we deliver. Deep down, we all know that science alone is far too narrow to truly define the mysteries and miracles of life.

Many of us feel close to mystery and miracles at certain times of the year or when events around us wake us up from time to time. But it would do us all some good to recognize the presence of both in our daily work. The sense of awe, wonder, and humility that such recognition brings can make us grateful. It maybe gives us some perspective when things with our patients either go very wrong or very right. At the end of each precious day, perhaps a one line expression of thanks from Florence Scovel Shinn is in order: "Today is a day of completion; I give thanks for this perfect day, miracle shall follow miracle and wonders shall never cease."

November

Suggested Reading

Articles

Huynh, Geraldine, et al. "Miracles in Medicine: A Narrative Inquiry Exploring Extraordinary Events in Pediatrics." *Health Science Reports,* vol. 6, no. 11, 8 Nov. 2023.

Books

Shinn, Florence Scovel. *The Game of Life and How to Play It.* DeVorss & Company, 1925.

Woodward, Kenneth L. *The Book of Miracles: The Meaning of the Miracle Stories in Christianity, Judaism, Buddhism, Hinduism, Islam.* Simon & Schuster, 2000.

PILGRIM

Pilgrimage

I love hiking. I love it because it can be a time of solitude and contemplation, a time when you can get lost in the rhythm of walking and solve problems, get perspective, and feel inspired and creative. Sometimes it can be a time to get to know someone better. Hiking often feels like a safe place to tell stories or share concerns we might not otherwise feel free to talk about. Hiking can give you a glimpse of the majesty of creation or reveal something new about the ordinary. It encourages gratitude for the world around us that we too often ignore. Hiking removes us, at least for a moment in time, from the treadmill of work and technology and the endless logistics of daily life.

With time to think on a recent hiking trip, it occurred to me that I might love medicine for many of the same reasons. Like many of you, I love medicine because of the connection it gives me with patients and the people I work with. In that sense, it is like I am on a very long hike with them, a road we share that creates a bond unique to what we do in those relationships. It is like we are on a road together—hopefully a healing road for both of us.

Nurturing the doctor-patient relationship is critical to keeping both patient and doctor emotionally healthy and fully engaged in achieving optimal medical care. This relationship can be a moving target in a rapidly evolving healthcare environment with the rise of medical consumerism, publicly posted patient reviews, and the ease at which our patients can research and become more active participants in medical decision-making. But none of that really changes the basic tenets of how we should approach our patients. The basics are the same as they have been for centuries. Ethicist Paul Ramsey described it well: "The practice of medicine is one such covenant. Justice, fairness, righteousness, faithfulness, canons of loyalty, the sanctity of life, *hesed, agape,* or charity are some of the names given to the moral quality of attitude and of action owed to all men by any man who steps into a covenant with another . . .

[It] explicitly acknowledges that we are a covenant people on a common pilgrimage." Whether viewed through a religious or secular lens, and masculine pronouns set aside, the idea is clear and gives us an admittedly idealized view of the doctor-patient relationship, but one nevertheless worth remembering.

What are the key ingredients in visibly honoring this relationship? In recent years, a great deal of emphasis has been placed on the level of empathy that is both heartfelt and tangibly evident when a physician cares for a patient. There is great truth in this; a sense of understanding, of "shared suffering" is indeed what we all need to different degrees throughout our lives. In his landmark article, "The Nature of Suffering and the Goals of Medicine," Eric Cassell notes, "The relief of suffering and the cure of the disease must be seen as two obligations of a medical profession that is truly dedicated to the care of the sick." Others have noted that although empathy is an essential characteristic of a holistic physician, it can be a two-edged sword that, when unbalanced or overdeveloped, can affect objectivity and judgment; it can be a significant contributor to physician burnout.

Empathy is a laudable goal, but a more basic understanding of the relationship between physicians and patients might just involve kindness. Kindness is hard to define, but easy to recognize. When you think about it, kindness encompasses all the critical components of covenant that Ramsey wrote about a half century ago. The more I have thought about kindness and now try to write about it, the more I realize how far short of it I fall most days, and how often I see and admire it in my colleagues, including my own doctors. It is true that we remember less about what someone said to us than how they made us feel when they said it. Kindness is a special quality that palpably conveys gentleness, generosity, and compassion. It's easy to find yourself in a hurry or frustrated, ignoring the shared humanity, even suffering in its many forms right there in front of us. We can fail in that moment to fully honor that covenant, that common pilgrimage physicians and patients take together. Perhaps intentionally honoring that higher calling more often might just be the difference between loving our work and just having a job.

The essence of our work, and how well we do it, comes down to healing the sick and hopefully ourselves along the way. When this partnership is fully realized, it is a partnership of love and trust. Each step in the long pilgrimage that is our life in medicine hopefully brings us new wisdom, patience, and connection with our patients, even though there are certainly obstacles on that road. The legacy that we slowly mold on that pilgrimage, then leave behind after a long career in medicine, may in part be defined by our diagnostic or therapeutic acumen. However in a more lasting sense, when I consider colleagues and mentors through the decades, their legacies are mostly defined by the ways they exhibit bonds with their patients and colleagues: patience, fidelity, empathy, love, and especially kindness. Yes. Kindness. That just might be enough.

Suggested Reading

Articles

Cassel, E.J. "The Nature of Suffering and the Goals of Medicine." *New England Journal of Medicine*, vol. 306, no. 11, 18 Mar. 1982, pp. 639-645.

Truog, Robert D. "Patients and Doctors—The Evolution of

a Relationship." *New England Journal of Medicine*, vol. 366, no. 7, 16 Feb. 2022, pp. 581-585.

Books

Ramsey, Paul. *The Patient as Person: Explorations in Medical Ethics*. Yale University Press, 1970.

Poetry

Nye, Naomi Shihab. "Kindness." *Words Under the Words: Selected Poems*, Greenwillow Books, 1995.

Whyte, David. "Camino." *Pilgrim*, Many Rivers Press, 2012.

Sacred Stories

Rantidevs's Compassion and Selflessness

Finisterre

Frederick Hudson championed a theory of cyclic change that recurs throughout adult life. These are life transitions, some of which are seismic and deeply desired; these visibly change our life trajectory. More often though, change is subtle, and we don't always recognize when or where we might be residing on Hudson's cycle of change at any given time. This can sometimes create an uneasiness that we can't quite put our finger on. Hudson describes four phases in the cycle of change: go for it, the doldrums, cocooning, and getting ready. In the "go for it" phase, life seems to be working, and there is a sense of purpose, of being on course. At some point though, a certain stagnation inevitably emerges in work, relationships, recreation, or particularly, in spiritual health. Such feelings are inevitable and are the gateway to the doldrums.

The doldrums is an ancient mariner's term for what is now referred to as the "inter-tropical convergence zone," a wandering area around the equator where the northern and southern trade winds collide. This creates an area where there may be eerily calm seas and no wind for weeks at a time. It was the bane of ancient explorers, whalers, and merchant ships that could be stuck there indefinitely—bored, restless, irritable, anxious. Coleridge famously described it in "The Rime of the Ancient Mariner":

> Day after day, day after day,
> We stuck, nor breath,
> nor motion;
> As idle as a painted ship
> Upon a painted ocean.

Sound familiar? In the cycle of change, the doldrums are downtime, a period of decline and malaise, but also they can be a new beginning to enact change. So, while the doldrums can be boring, they serve a purpose and are the gateway to the next phase, cocooning. In cocooning, we enter a phase of transformation. This is an emotional period where we can reflect on the past and look forward to the future. It may be a long period of sabbatical or a series of short breaks, where we explore what form the process of renewal will take for us and where it might lead. Like the butterfly in a cocoon, it may not look like much, but within the cocoon, there is deep work occurring, and with time and patience, something new will emerge.

In the days after my father died when I was twelve years old, someone sent us a beautiful letter that I still remember the essence of, though not the exact wording—that with death we enter a cocoon that allows us, like the butterfly, to transform into something more beautiful, eternal, and free of the worries of this life. As a child, it was comforting enough that all these years later I still remember it, and I still think of it whenever I see a cocoon. As an adult, I think it sticks with me because I realize now that, with grieving, a transformation was occurring, as the adolescent version of me prepared for a life altered by that loss. Even then, there were cycles of change.

Significant change is seldom easy, even when urgently needed or forced upon us, let alone when it must be discerned and unfold with uncertainty.

The process, even with defined stages, often involves a certain mystery. Gaining something new always requires giving up something old, something that no longer quite works. Indeed, our mental well-being and happiness depend on our perpetual capacity for change, on allowing the process to unfold with humility and patience, on living in the present while imagining a future ... on letting the past be the past. The reward is one of the mountaintops of life, where change is realized, acted on, and becomes fully visible.

Nearing the end of a long career, my children now adults with families of their own, I spent a couple of weeks walking the last stages of the Camino de Santiago thru Galicia in northern Spain. It's an ancient religious/spiritual pilgrimage that ends at the Cathedral in Santiago de Compostela, where relics of St. James rest near the altar. For many, the pilgrimage continues from there westward another sixty miles to Finisterre, where Spain meets the sea, a place the ancients believed to be the "end of the world."

As you begin your Camino, you're told to carry a stone, wherein you place your "ghosts," the things or people you mourn, regrets, things lost along the way, trauma, whatever you need to set down on an inward journey to wholeness, and somewhere along the Camino, you leave the stone behind. Discovering your ghosts is an integral part of the pilgrimage, and the road itself brings a flood of memories longing to be put into perspective. All along the Camino at wayfinding markers, there are stones that fellow *peregrinos* have set down, making room for something new. Finding discernment slow, I held mine all the way to Finisterre, where I went to the edge of the tall cliff below the lighthouse and threw my stone into the sea. What that will lead to remains to be seen ... but I am hopeful.

Suggested Reading

Books

Hudson, Frederick. *The Handbook of Coaching: A Comprehensive Resource Guide for Managers, Executives, Consultants, and Human Resource Professionals.* Jossey-Bass, 1999.

Poetry

Coleridge, Samuel Taylor. "The Rime of the Ancient Mariner." *Lyrical Ballads,* J. & A. Arch, 1798.

Machado, Antonio. "Traveler, There Is No Road." *Selected Poems of Antonio Machado*, translated by Betty Jean Craige, Louisiana State University Press, 1979.

Whyte, David. "Finisterre." *Pilgrim*, Many Rivers Press, 2012.

Afterword

In September and October of 2023, I walked the final stages of the Camino de Santiago with a dozen people I had never laid eyes on until that first morning, people of all ages, from all over the world.

Somehow, the very act of being on a pilgrimage bound us together almost immediately. We were open and generous; we extended each other the grace to ignore quirks and annoyances. It's funny how easy it was to see that commonality in that environment and how hard it is for most people to fully embrace it back in the real world.

Our days on the trail quickly developed a rhythm. We shared a communal breakfast and started on the trail as a group of a dozen or so, slowly breaking into groups of two or three. Mornings were punctuated with the constant crowing of roosters urging us on. We talked about all kinds of things, mostly about our lives back home. In doing so, we slowly developed a bond that naturally led us to confide, to listen, and to be heard, often about things that had brought twelve very different people to a pilgrimage. Hearing and being heard ... something so simple and yet so powerful.

We'd stop along the way for lunch, usually in some small village. After lunch, our paces varied greatly, some speeding ahead, others slogging along in need of a nap. We tended to walk alone some in the afternoons, often connecting for long or short conversations with other *peregrinos*, strangers from all over the world whose paths we seemed to silently cross frequently, randomly, day after day until it seemed natural to strike up a conversation. Walking alone brought time to reflect, to drop into ancient churches, or to pause at outdoor cafes. The trail threaded through villages, lush farmlands, backyard kale gardens, and cattle farms. It was not unusual to have to navigate past cats or chickens or occasional goats.

Sometimes the scenery was breathtaking, and I often sat on one of many ancient stone walls that lined the trail to take it in. It was a lesson in awareness of my own thoughts, of prayer, and an unusually keen recognition of the natural world and its inhabitants, most living very simple lives. I wondered what it would be like to live such a simple, rural life. I pondered if it would be a purer existence, or just different, something made surprisingly complex by hard work, poverty, and lack of access to good healthcare and larger opportunity. By late afternoon, we would all gradually straggle in over an hour or more at a café, eating all kinds of food and drinking far too much wine or Estrella Galicia beer.

Part of the experience was an unexpectedly meaningful connection with these fellow travelers, becoming so close for days. Then suddenly they, along with that closeness and confidence, were ... gone. We all scattered to the wind on that last night after the emotional Botafumeiro Mass in the Cathedral and a last dinner together. It caused a palpable ache for weeks, and I still feel a sense of grief when I look at the pictures and wonder what became of them. It made me realize that in a long lifetime so many people come and go from our lives and how precious, what a gift it is, to have close friends and family who are there to stay, who know your story and know when to listen or reach out.

It has been much the same practicing medicine all these years. I still remember patients who became close family, as well as professors, fellow interns and residents, and older doctors who mentored me early in my career. There have been so many people who helped me along in my career and taught me how to care for patients and our colleagues. Many of them have retired or died, or in other ways moved out of my life, but I carry them with me still, nowadays making a conscious effort to remember them and what I learned from them. The older and further into my career I get, the more I value these connections, past and present.

One afternoon, after a lunch that was too big and with the sun beating down on me, to get off my feet and out of the heat, I stepped into the Church of St. Julian de Moraime near Muxia. It's an ancient church and monastery dating back to the 12th century, sacked by Norman pirates, then the Saxons, before it was restored by fourteen-year-old King Alfonso of Galicia. Like most of the other ancient churches along the Camino, it was built from large stones and was cool, quiet, and dark inside. I sat for a while and prayed. I soon found myself lost in thought.

I noticed the only other person in the church that afternoon was an elderly lady who couldn't weigh more than ninety pounds. She was struggling to get up from the pew using a tall walking stick. She was obviously a local, in a simple dark cotton dress, her sandals worn to the point of falling apart. I noticed her hands showed pronounced deformities of rheumatoid arthritis, and once on her feet, she walked with very short shuffling strides as she left the church. As a rheumatologist, I couldn't help but be sad about the difficulties she must have endured all those years, almost certainly without adequate medical care.

Another day, there was an elderly Australian man I walked with slowly for about an hour, then sat with for a snack. He kept me fascinated with stories of his life as a bar owner in Sydney. He was an engaging guy who had severe arthritis in his knees. He walked slowly using two canes, but was determined to walk at least the last hundred kilometers of the Camino as he had dreamed of doing throughout his life. There were other infirmities I noticed—in particular, one healthy-appearing young woman with a glucose monitor on her upper arm who passed by several times in those days.

It occurred to me, at some point that without intending to, I was looking through the lens of a physician as I passed by or interacted with other *peregrinos*. I felt at times an overwhelming impulse to help them. We all have certain biases and ways of looking at the world, and physicians are no different. Walking on that road was a great equalizer. We were all sharing a pilgrimage, though we all encountered it with different perspectives, different baggage, different desires.

It may be that those days on the trail were life changing because it completely removed me from the day-to-day. It isolated me, gave me time to think, to remember things and people from the past, to connect with new people with whom I shared no baggage, to release regrets, to search for my faith and to realize that I am so very blessed. Most of all, by the end, I felt a deep, intense sense of gratitude that even now I find difficult to fully describe.

I had a lot of time on the trail to think about

my career and medicine in general. My formative years in medicine were sandwiched between two great transitions of modern medicine. I was blessed to come after the "Golden Age of Medicine"—the first half of the 20th century that brought the miracles of antibiotics, immunizations, improved surgical techniques, and other breakthrough treatments that seemed primitive now but saved countless lives then. My career will likely end with the current state of medicine that *New Yorker* writer Dhruv Khullar calls the "Gilded Age of Medicine," in which corporate medicine and the bottom line rule the day, challenging us with great obstacles to still bring patience and kindness and healing to our patients. As tragic and challenging as that change has been, I've been able to practice in an era where autoimmune diseases, cancer, AIDS, diabetes, heart disease, and so many other conditions are now preventable, curable, or able to be controlled. When I think of the suffering and ruined lives we witnessed in the 1980s, and now see people with these same diseases living normal lives, I can scarcely believe the miracles that have taken place are now expected as routine. For many of the corporate and venture capital groups that now own and manage practices and those who insure the lives that we treat, the focus has largely shifted to science and economics. Our most foundational calling—to connect and try to heal rather than just cure our patients—is at once easier to ignore and more vital to honor. It is the defining expression of individual ethics and our sense of calling that we must tangibly honor each day we spend with patients, with every step on the pilgrimage we share with them.

As was the case in the many seasons of my life, each with its own unique terrain—childhood, medicine, seminary, marriage, parenthood, and so many other roads—the version of me that came to the end of the Camino was different than the person who entered it. So many roads that we take in life change us, for better or worse, all converging on one long road, one sacred pilgrimage of life.

The long road we travel during our lives in medicine, and beyond, is a road of transformation, a road of giving and receiving healing, an endless road without a final destination in our brief lifetime here. What we do in this world, the world St. Augustine called the "City of Man," is sacred and changes the lives of those we love and care for. Where the road ultimately leads is a matter of personal belief, a destination that none of us can be entirely certain of. Faith tells me that what we do in this world matters, but the road continues beyond this world, a road that leads to the eternal City of God. In church each week, we sing the reassuring close to the Gloria Patri:

> *As it was in the beginning,*
> *is now, and ever shall be:*
> *world without end.*
> *Amen.*

And so, our pilgrimage down the healing road continues to the horizon and beyond, grace and love, faith and blessings nourishing us as we go.

Suggested Reading

Articles

Khullar, Dhruv. "The Gilded Age of Medicine Is Here." *The New Yorker,* 12 Dec. 2024.

Acknowledgments

Sharing the stories and lessons from a career in medicine has made me realize just how many people have touched my life, influenced me, and taught me lessons throughout the years. The process of writing these stories in what I hope is a coherent narrative proved far more challenging than I would have imagined, and it has only deepened my appreciation for everyone who has helped me along the way.

As I have written these essays, memories of those who guided me through my training have come flooding back - along with vivid flashes of the moments and lessons I associate with each of them. When I picture the professors and clinicians who shaped my medical school and residency years, their faces and personalities remain frozen in time. Still the stories, the skills they taught me, and the wisdom they imparted feel as alive as ever. Although I'm still in touch with a handful of my fellow students and residents, most are relegated to memory. What stands out most from those relationships are the support and friendship we offered one another during years that were some of the best and most challenging of our lives. Looking back at those formative experiences - and the people who meant so much to me - makes me grateful for what an extraordinary time of life it was when the mystery and wonder of medicine was so tangible as we delivered babies, scrubbed for surgery, or took care of a critically ill patient for the first time.

I have practiced my entire 40-year career in Austin at the same hospital and in the office building. I have lost count as to how many colleagues have taught me things, pitched in to help me with my patients, encouraged me, trusted me with their patients and family, laughed with me, have been frustrated alongside me, and commiserated with me. These are precious memories, and they remind me just how essential a community of colleagues is - both for making each day more manageable and rewarding, and for ensuring that your patients are well cared for. Most of the colleagues I started with have retired now, and I am not far behind, but new generations have stepped in to carry the work forward. They are part of the long lineage of medicine and I find myself learning just as much, if not more, from my younger colleagues today.

For many years I have worked in our medical society's programs for physician wellness, counseling, and with those in recovery. These have been rewarding years. The programs have accomplished much, but like any volunteer mission, I have received much more than I have given. Among those gifts have been colleagues who have supported these programs and, in the process, become close friends: Jenny, Claire, and Christy to name a few, though there are many others. These transformative programs have been made possible by dedicated members of our staff who have been kind and loyal to me and our mission, and who creatively make our programs so effective.

A career in medicine, particularly in the era I have practiced, exacts a toll on any physician's family, causing them to make sacrifices they didn't necessarily sign up for and can seldom control. I wish my patients knew that those expedited visits, evening and weekend pages, and hospital care visits could only take place because of the kindness and understanding of my family. Nothing has kept the wind in my sails, often at their expense, more than my wife Maryann and my children, now grown and with children of their own.

I am grateful to my publisher, Brooke, for her patience and for making me appear to be a better writer than I am. Her guidance helped mold these stories into something I am truly proud of. To Meg who has guided me through the publishing process with patience and wisdom, and to Meghan who had the unfortunate role of copyeditor and had to endure strange and repetitive errors that I should have known to avoid since Mrs. Becker's 7th grade English class.

Last but not least, I am deeply grateful to my patients - some of whom I began seeing nearly half a century ago, when we were all just kids, and who have since become friends, many almost like family. From them, I have learned more lessons about medicine and life than I can possibly count. They have made each day we were together a precious gift.

www.ingramcontent.com/pod-product-compliance
Lightning Source LLC
LaVergne TN
LVHW091711070526
838199LV00050B/2344